THE MESSIAH

Final Events of His Earthly Journey

DR. FRED STAPLETON

This panoramic view of the life of Christ is a true journey of wonder and amazement. As you read the pages of this book literally following the steps of Jesus, you will find a wealth of unparalleled truth. Each chapter draws you close to His inner circle. THE MESSIAH will provide a great devotion as well as theological explanations. Now, let's join Dr. Stapleton on this blessed journey.

—Dr. Zackary L. Sizemore, D.Th., D.Min
President of Piedmont College of Theology
China Grove, North Carolina

I am so thankful for the privilege of working with Bro. Fred Stapleton on his book, THE MESSIAH—Final Events of His Earthly Journey. It takes a deep dive into the details of Christ's final days on earth and shares many powerful insights that will speak to your soul. He explains things from the Jewish cultural customs of Jesus' time that make the Scriptures come alive with fresh meaning. Having ministered with Bro. Fred several times, I know his heart and love for people and his passion to share the Gospel with the world. In THE MESSIAH, the pure Gospel message rings true and comes through loud and clear. This book will lead you to a deeper encounter with Christ, give you a better understanding of His sacrifice, and create a greater appetite for His Word. Both the titles "Christ" and "Messiah" mean "the anointed One." The anointing of the Holy Spirit rests on the author of this book and the message it contains. As you read it, that anointing will be transferred to you. Be ready to receive a spiritual impartation.

—Ben Godwin, B.Th.
Pastor, Author
Goodsprings Full Gospel Church
Goodsprings, Alabama

I have long awaited the day that Apostle Stapleton would write his first book! I know firsthand of the great knowledge that he has acquired in a lifetime of walking in intimacy with Jesus. He downloads this to you firsthand in his new book THE MESSIAH. THE MESSIAH will open your eyes to see the life and ministry of Jesus in a whole new light. You will feel like you are literally walking the streets of the Holy Land with Jesus firsthand. It is able to challenge the minds of the learned, yet it is still written in a way that the new believer can understand. It will impact you in your personal walk with Christ for years to come!

—Pastor Seth Avery
Living Hope Tabernacle
Lenoir, North Carolina

I know this man. I have known few men who so passionately love Jesus that it manifests in every aspect of their life. I met Fred in a diner in North Carolina. He was sitting behind me so I couldn't see his face, but I could hear his voice and I knew at once that this was a man who loves Jesus. That love for the Lord Jesus has never been on more vivid display than in this book, THE MESSIAH—Final Events of His Earthly Journey. If you already love Jesus, you will love Him more as you read this book. Thank you Fred Stapleton—you have blessed me more than you can know.

—Michael Gantt
Pastor, Author, Missionary

It was only after I became acquainted with the Lord Jesus Christ that I truly valued His Word. When I met Him as my Savior, His Word became a lamp unto my feet and a light unto my path. In like manner, I have been blessed to walk with Freddie Stapleton for over 30 years. I have never known a more selfless, compassionate, sincere, mission-minded man of God. That makes me value His biblical insights and revelations from God. What shaped his character will surely help to shape mine. What awakened the anointing and the gifts of the Holy Spirit in his life will surely awaken the anointing and the gifts of the Spirit in mine. What empowers him to overcome in life will surely empower me to overcome as well. That's why Paul wrote the Philippians and told them that they were all "partakers" of his grace (Ph. 1:7). What God does in one, he delights to transfer to another. As you read this wonderful account of the final days of the Messiah on the earth, the grace of many revelations will crash over your soul—like waves of glory—especially the insights that connect the Church to our Abrahamic roots. One of the most valuable truths my dear brother in the Lord has imparted to me concerned that very insight—when he invited me to go to Israel for the Feast of Tabernacles. I will always be indebted to him for that, and now our company (Deeper Revelation Books) has the privilege of publishing this book. What a blessing!

—Mike Shreve, B.Th., D.Div.
Evangelist, Pastor, Author, Publisher
Cleveland, Tennessee

This book! It is what it is: a sum of knowledge and understanding of the life of Jesus that Dr. Stapleton has transmitted on paper. In an inspirational way, the author also details some biblical languages that portrays the similarity between Jesus in the Old Testament and Jesus in the New Testament.

—Dr. Marc A Brice
Retired Social Studies Teacher
Founder of Caribbean Christian Club
Haiti Missions Service

Fred Stapleton's, *The Messiah*, is a powerful treatise on the life of Jesus, especially the last hours of the journey to the cross. This work is what I call "a living commentary." The reader will not only learn from the author's vast knowledge of Jewish custom but will glean valuable insight for everyday life in our modern times. Dr. Fred's authenticity shines through in this work and allows him to speak with humble authority as a servant leader! You will be blessed by this work! Get ready to know Jesus more intimately as you read and study, *The Messiah*.

—Pastor Keith Nix, B.BS., M.Min., D.Min.
The Lift Church
Sevierville, Tennessee

THE MESSIAH—Final Events of His Earthly Journey
Copyright © 2020 Dr. Fred Stapleton
ISBN: 978-1-949297-35-5
LCCN: 2020922363

All rights reserved. No part of this book may be reproduced, stored in a retrieval system, or transmitted in any form or by any means—electronic, mechanical, digital, photocopy, or any other—without prior permission from the publisher and author, except as provided by the United States of America copyright law.

All Scripture references are from the KING JAMES VERSION of the Bible, public domain.

Honorary Degree: Because of his many years of devotion to ministry, missions, and building the local church, in 2017, Fred Stapleton was awarded a Doctor of Ministry degree by Piedmont College of Theology.

Address all personal correspondence to:
Dr. Fred Stapleton
Cornerstone Covenant World Missions
P.O. Box 488
Hudson, N.C. 28638
Phone: 828-387-0646
Email: freddiestapleton12@gmail.com

Individuals and church groups may order books from Fred Stapleton directly, or from the publisher. Retailers and wholesalers should order from our distributors. Refer to the Deeper Revelation Books website for distribution information, as well as an online catalog of all our books.

Published by:
Deeper Revelation Books
Revealing "the deep things of God" (1 Cor. 2:10)
P.O. Box 4260 Cleveland, TN 37320
Phone: 423-478-2843
Website: www.deeperrevelationbooks.org
Email: info@deeperrevelationbooks.org

Cover artwork:
"Foot Washing" by Yongsung Kim. Havenlight.com

Deeper Revelation Books assists Christian authors in publishing and distributing their books. Final responsibility for design, content, permissions, editorial accuracy, and doctrinal views, either expressed or implied, belongs to the author.

CONTENTS

CHAPTER 1
The Last Supper (John 13) 15

CHAPTER 2
The Marriage Covenant (John 14) 33

CHAPTER 3
Jesus—The True Vine (John 15) 49

CHAPTER 4
Walking and Talking with Jesus (John 16) 67

CHAPTER 5
Jesus Talks to His Daddy (John 17) 83

CHAPTER 6
Jesus Drinks the Cup of Wrath (John 18) 99

CHAPTER 7
The Crucifixion of Jesus (John 19) 117

CHAPTER 8
Jesus' Seven Statements from the Cross 141

CHAPTER 9
The Resurrection (John 20) 163

CHAPTER 10
The Restoration of Peter (John 21) 183

CHAPTER 11
The Kingdom of God (Acts 1) 199

CHAPTER 12
Pentecost and Beyond (Acts 2) 219

CONCLUSION
By Brad Bartlett 243

PHOTO GALLERY 247

ACKNOWLEDGMENTS

Connie and I would like to express our deepest appreciation to our parents, John and Reba Hicks, Otis Adams, and Mary Fleenor, for teaching us about Jesus.

Our deepest love and appreciation go out to our four beautiful daughters, Hannah, Danielle, Priscilla, and Bekah. All of you have brought great joy into our lives. To our precious grandchildren, Parker, David, Braxton, Aliyah, Brooklyn, Kolton, Dezlyn, and Journey, you are each a great treasure to us.

Our heartfelt thanks go out to Pastor Danny and Judy Honeycutt, Assistant Pastor Tony and Lisa English, Elders and Staff, and the amazing Congregation of Cornerstone Covenant Church for all your years of love and support.

We would like to express our sincere gratitude to our spiritual parents in the Lord, Dr. Bahjat and Dr. Nina Batarseh of Way of Light Ministries, the late David Eugene and Goldie Stines, and his son, the late Jesse Stines and Kathy Stines of Blue Ridge Mountain Church, and the late Clyde and Betty Avery of Living Hope Tabernacle. Your love and influence in our lives has made this book possible.

Our deepest appreciation goes to Cornerstone Covenant World Missions and the Ambassadors for your love and support. Also, to our many ministerial friends all over the world. We love all of you Pastors and Ministers who are serving God faithfully.

Our sincere appreciation goes to Brad Bartlett for

teaming up with us. His input into this book was of great value.

Our great appreciation goes to Mike Shreve and his staff of Deeper Revelation Books, especially Vicki Henley and Ben Godwin. You have made this book the best it can be for the Lord Jesus Christ.

Most importantly, our sincere gratitude goes to our Lord and Savior, Jesus Christ. For the communion and leadership of the Holy Spirit in writing this book. There are not enough words to adequately acknowledge all Jesus has done for us. We love Him most because He loved us first!

DEDICATION

This book is dedicated in memory of my special friend, Anthony James Rogers. We shared a special bond and a mutual love. He would ask his mom to bring him to Campmeeting to see me and hear me preach. Anthony touched many lives during his sixteen years with us. He had an infectious smile and was able to communicate through his joyful smile. Anthony developed special bonds with many people, including me, his parents, family members, and friends. He had a special way with people and enjoyed spending time with them. While we will always grieve his loss, we are happy knowing that Anthony is now walking and talking with our heavenly Father.

Anthony James Rogers
12/16/2001–11/18/2018

INTRODUCTION

Thank you for choosing to read this book. My heart's desire for you as you read and study this book is to discover a greater understanding of what Jesus did for you on the last day of His life and what He is still doing for you since His Resurrection. My prayer for you as you study the Word of God contained in this book, is that you will discovery treasures of truth which will increase your faith and empower your walk with the Lord. Job 28:1 says, *"Surely there is a vein* [a mine] *for the silver, and a place for gold where they fine* [refine] *it."* The majority of silver and gold is not found on the surface of the earth. You have to dig below the surface to find the true treasures.

I have been digging for truth and a greater understanding of God's Word for over 50 years. During that time, the Lord has honored my heart's desire by surrounding me with mentors—great men of God whom I respect for their love and wise council, such as Pastor David Gene Stines and Dr. Bahjat Batarseh.

God's glory is concealed in His Word but Proverbs 25:2 declares, *"It is the glory of God to conceal a thing: but the honour of kings is to search out a matter."* In this book we will dig out and search out many treasures which are hidden under the surface of Scripture. We will look over a vast treasure trove of truth concerning the last day of Jesus' earthly ministry and the events immediately following His resurrection. These events and truths reveal to us the intentions of our Lord as He empowers us to fulfill His Great Commission.

Get your book and pen and let's go on a spiritual treasure hunt together! You will surely uncover things even beyond what I share with you. We love you. We pray blessings to you and to the "sheep" of your individual pastures.

CHAPTER 1

THE LAST SUPPER
(John 13)

This chapter and the following chapters will take us through the last day of Jesus' life. They will take you through the events of His last day recorded in chapters 13-17 of the Gospel of John. If you have a red-letter edition Bible, these five chapters are almost totally filled with red ink, indicating the words of Jesus. My desire is to highlight the price Jesus paid on our behalf to cover our sin debt. My hope is for the reader to fully understand the connection between sin and its consequences. Jesus Christ led a pure and sinless life, a life of loving obedience and unwavering devotion to His Father. I hope you will fully grasp what Jesus did for you on His last day. Jesus had a perfect understanding of the terrible price sin exacts of the sinner. He had to know that price, because He had committed from the foundation of the world to pay it in full. We hope to demonstrate how He paid it in full for us. Also, how He was preparing the disciples to carry on His ministry after His Ascension.

The day begins with the Last Supper and will end with Jesus being suspended between heaven and earth on the cross as the sin bearer of all mankind. Before the sun sets again, He would breathe His last breath. In the Jewish tradition, days follow the pattern of night first, then daytime.

Still today, practicing Jews observe the Sabbath beginning at sunset on Friday and ending at sunset on Saturday. Luke 23:44-46 records, *"And it was about the sixth hour, and there was a darkness over all the earth until the ninth hour. And the sun was darkened, and the veil of the temple was rent in the midst. And when Jesus had cried with a loud voice, he said, Father, into thy hands I commend my spirit: and having said thus, he gave up the ghost."* Jesus died at the 9th hour or 3:00 in the afternoon; also known as the "Hour of Prayer."

John chapters 13-17 has become known as the "Upper Room Discourse." In these five chapters, Jesus was preparing Himself for His trial and crucifixion and preparing His disciples for the ministry that was before them—to go into all the world and make disciples. He was preparing them for the Great Commission. Jesus was preparing them to be future leaders as apostles in His kingdom and church. In the book of John, chapters 1-12, John wrote about Jesus from the beginning of eternity. In fact, in the very first verse of His Gospel John revealed Jesus' divinity and true identity. *"In the beginning was the Word, and the Word was with God, and the Word was God"* (John 1:1). Then John recorded His birth, *"And **the Word was made flesh**, and dwelt among us, (and we beheld his glory, the glory as of the only begotten of the Father,) full of grace and truth"* (John 1:14). The first twelve chapters of John leads us to the Upper Room. In the five chapters of John 13-17, Jesus revealed His heart to these disciples. He was

> *Jesus was preparing Himself for His trial and crucifixion and preparing His disciples for the ministry that was before them.*

preparing them to carry the ministry He brought to the earth to all the nations. The crowds were gone, the seventy part-time disciples walked away, and Jesus was only left with the original twelve and one of them will betray Him.

Before we study John 13, let's set the stage by looking at Luke 22:23-24, *"And they began to enquire among themselves, which of them it was that should do this thing. And there was also a strife among them,* **which of them should be accounted the greatest**.*"* Now examine John 13:1, *"Now before the feast of the passover, when Jesus knew that his hour was come that he should depart out of this world unto the Father, having loved his own which were in the world, he loved them unto the end."*

While Jesus was facing death, the disciples' only concern was for themselves. They were arguing over positions in the kingdom—*"And when the ten heard it, they began to be much displeased with James and John"* (Mark 10:41). The Scripture says there was strife among them, so the argument was heated. This wasn't the first time this issue came up. Notice Mark 9:33-34, *"And he came to Capernaum: and being in the house he asked them, What was it that ye disputed among yourselves by the way? But they held their peace: for by the way they had disputed among themselves,* **who should be the greatest**.*"* Luke 9:46 agrees, *"Then there arose a reasoning among them,* **which of them should be greatest**.*"*

One of the more detailed descriptions of this struggle to be the greatest is found in Matthew 20:20-26, *"Then came to him the mother of Zebedee's children with her sons, worshipping him, and desiring a certain thing of him. And he said unto her, What wilt thou? She saith unto him,* **Grant that these my two sons may sit, the one on thy**

right hand, and the other on the left, in thy kingdom. *But Jesus answered and said, Ye know not what ye ask. Are ye able to drink of the cup that I shall drink of, and to be baptized with the baptism that I am baptized with? They say unto him, We are able. And he saith unto them, Ye shall drink indeed of my cup, and be baptized with the baptism that I am baptized with: but to sit on my right hand, and on my left, is not mine to give, but it shall be given to them for whom it is prepared of my Father. And **when the ten heard it, they were moved with indignation against the two brethren**. But Jesus called them unto him, and said, Ye know that the princes of the Gentiles exercise dominion over them, and they that are great exercise authority upon them. But it shall not be so among you: but **whosoever will be great among you, let him be your minister.**"* We are going to see how Jesus dealt with their arguing with one another. No one who is about to die wants their family to be arguing.

John 13:1 reads, *"Now before the feast of the passover, when Jesus knew that his hour was come that he should depart out of this world unto the Father, having loved his own which were in the world, he loved them unto the end."* This verse tells us Jesus loves them all, which included Judas Iscariot. He loved them all to the very end.

How the heart of Jesus must have been broken. Luke 19:41-44 informs us He was already brokenhearted over Jerusalem—*"And when he was come near, he beheld the city, **and wept over it**, Saying, If thou hadst known, even thou, at least in this thy day, the things which belong unto thy peace! but now they are hid from thine eyes. For the days shall come upon thee, that thine enemies* *shall cast a trench about thee, and compass thee round, and keep thee in on every side, And shall lay thee even with the ground, and thy children within thee; and they shall not leave in thee one stone upon another; because thou knewest not the time of thy visitation."*

This verse, John 13:1, reminds me of something my daughter, Priscilla, said while she was speaking to thousands in Haiti at the young age of sixteen. She said God spoke these words to her, "You keep messing up, but I (Jesus) will keep loving you." After these words, she closed her eyes, began to weep so hard, and began to pray in the Spirit. We saw so many miracles among those precious people in the next fifteen minutes. Many of the Haitians, for the first time, realized that Jesus would keep loving them until the end. Jesus demonstrated an act of love that the disciples had not understood before.

My daughter Priscilla (center).

The disciples saw leadership as power, influence, and having a platform to be elevated above others which can be essential. They didn't understand the servant side of leadership. You might climb to the top through ambition and hard work, but no leader can stay on top very long without a servant's heart. As ministers of the Gospel, we lead by serving others or we don't truly lead at all. Jesus knew His time had come to show His disciples the full extent of His love. He knew what He was facing in the hours to come, yet His only concern was for His disciples whom He loved absolutely to the end.

JESUS WASHES HIS DISCIPLE'S FEET

John 13:2-3 continues, *"And supper being ended, the devil having now put into the heart of Judas Iscariot, Simon's son, to betray him; Jesus knowing that the Father had given all things into his hands, and that he was come from God, and went to God."* Here was Jesus knowing that He had been given authority over all things and that He came from God and was going back to God. Then Jesus shocked them all by what He did next. John 13:4-17 paints the picture, *"He riseth from supper, and laid aside his garments; and took a towel, and girded himself. After that he poureth water into a bason, and began to wash the disciples' feet, and to wipe them with the towel wherewith he was girded. Then cometh he to Simon Peter: and Peter saith unto him, Lord, dost thou wash my feet? Jesus answered and said unto him, What I do thou knowest not now; but thou shalt know hereafter. Peter saith unto him, Thou shalt never wash my feet. Jesus answered him, If I wash thee not, thou hast no part with me. Simon Peter saith unto him, Lord, not my feet only, but also my hands and my head. Jesus saith to him, He that is washed needeth not save to wash his feet, but is clean every whit: and ye are clean, but not all. For he knew who should betray him; therefore said he, Ye are not all clean. So after he had washed their feet, and had taken his garments, and was set down again, he said unto them, Know ye what I have done to you? Ye call me Master and Lord: and ye say well; for so I am. If I then, your Lord and Master, have washed your feet; ye also ought to wash one another's feet. For I have given you an example, that ye should do as I have done to you. Verily, verily, I say unto you, The servant is not greater than his lord;*

neither he that is sent greater than he that sent him. If ye know these things, happy are ye if ye do them."

Jesus did something radical to teach them the most important lesson they needed as servant leaders of His earthly kingdom. This is the way Jesus always taught them, by His example and by modeling it before them. Acts 1:1 says, *"The former treatise have I made, O Theophilus, of all that Jesus began **both to do and teach**."* Jesus got up from the table and prepared Himself to wash the feet of His disciples. Here is the King of kings preparing to wash their filthy, stinky feet and then to dry them with a towel. Note in John 13:2, the verse starts out saying, *"And supper being ended."* Normally, they would have washed their feet before supper. Because no one was willing to humble themselves, they ate with filthy feet. The host had provided a pitcher of water and a basin but had not provided a servant to wash their feet. According to the customs of hospitality, a typical host would greet and kiss his guest, then offer a servant to wash the guest's feet or allow them to wash their own feet (see Luke 7:44-46).

> *Jesus did something radical to teach them the most important lesson they needed as servant leaders of His earthly kingdom.*

The host was apparently not present, I believe at the request of Jesus in order to more fully teach His disciples this valuable lesson. The disciples, it seems, were trying to decide who was the least, not just who was the greatest. Walking in sandals on the dusty roads of Israel, where animal dung littered the streets, made it imperative that people's feet be washed before they would eat a communal meal. They would be reclining on a pillow at a low table and their feet would be almost in someone else's face. Remember also, the devil had put in Judas' heart to betray Jesus, but Jesus, amazingly, was going to wash his feet too.

"Jesus knowing that the Father had given all things into his hands" (John 13:3). Jesus was getting ready to perform an act of humility with full consciousness of His supreme power. The next part of verse three says, *"And that he was come from God, and went to God."* He was fully aware of His divine origin and of the divine glory to which He was about to return. Being conscious of all this, He was about to demonstrate the greatest example of self-denial ever displayed. This is precisely the act of love that Jesus displayed to His disciples. Jesus settled the dispute over "which was the greatest among them." It was related to their unwillingness to perform the washing of each other's feet or even their own feet. So, He took a towel, and girded himself and began washing their feet. Jesus left His throne in Heaven and came to live among us as a servant. In the John 13:5-17 passage above, Jesus performed the work of the lowliest of servants. He began to wash the disciple's feet but when He came to Peter, Peter objected, *"Lord doest thou wash my feet?"* Peter was stunned at the act of humility that Christ, His Lord and Master, would wash his feet when it would have been more proper for them to wash Jesus' feet. But Jesus, even though He was King, came as a suffering servant.

Read Isaiah 58, which develops the idea found in Matthew 20:28 that, *"Even as the Son of man came not to be ministered unto, but to minister, and to give his life a ransom for many."* Because there were no servants present to wash their feet, Jesus stooped to do this lowly task Himself. They were all stunned into silence except Peter. Peter was uncomfortable with the Lord washing his feet, so he protested and said, *"Thou shalt never wash my feet."* Jesus responded, *"If I wash thee not, thou hast no part with Me."* Peter, who really loved Jesus, then requested a complete washing. Jesus knew their hearts were toward Him. Jesus was saying, "you have been washed by My Words," but as you walk through this world, your feet (your walk) will need to be washed again and again. We come to Jesus to be washed from our sins and to be saved. He cleanses us completely, but our feet, our walk, must be clean from the effects of living in a sin-cursed world. This is done by the Holy Spirit through the washing of water by the Word. The Word is given to equip us for every good work—*"All scripture is given by inspiration of God, and is profitable for doctrine, for reproof, for correction, for instruction in righteousness: That the man of God may be perfect,* **thoroughly furnished unto all good works**" (2 Timothy 3:16-17).

Jesus said in John 13:11, *"Ye are not all clean"* referring to Judas. When you are rebuked, don't contact another leader outside your leadership about it. That is exactly what Judas did. I will personally never criticize your Pastor with you. Notice that all the disciples were upset by Mary's act of worship not just Judas. Matthew 26:7 tells the story, *"There came unto him a woman having an alabaster box of precious ointment, and poured it on his head, as he sat at meat."*

If you look at Matthew 26:8-16, you'll find that all of the disciples were upset, but only one (Judas) went outside the group. Then in verse 15, notice the religious leaders of that day and Judas covenanted (conspired) together. This dashed Judas' hopes for political power and influence. Judas probably thought, *Why continue to follow Jesus when the whole world is turning against him.*

According to Mark 14:1-2, *"After two days was the feast of the passover, and of unleavened bread: and the chief priests and the scribes sought how they might take him by craft and put him to death. But they said, Not on the feast day, lest there be an uproar of the people."* Satan did all this without possessing Judas because it wasn't until after Jesus gave him bread that Satan entered into Judas. Be careful how you respond to a rebuke. Judas opened the door to demonic influences because he rebelled against Jesus' correction. *"**And after the sop Satan entered into him**. Then said Jesus unto him, That thou doest, do quickly"* (John 13:27).

Jesus said in John 13:15, *"For I have given you **an example**, that ye should do as I have done to you."* We are to serve one another in lowliness of heart and mind, seeking to build one another in humility and love. When we seek the preeminence, we displease the Lord. When we have servant's heart, the Lord promised we would be happy (blessed)—*"If ye know these things, **happy are ye if ye do them**"* (John 13:17).

In John 13:7, *"Jesus answered [Peter] and said unto him, What I do thou knowest not now; but thou shalt know hereafter."* They didn't perceive what Jesus was doing then, but they understood later. Jesus was getting ready to go back to His throne. At that point, they only saw Jesus the Messiah as a prophet, teacher, and king, but not as a priest. Let's look at Hebrew 8:4, *"For if he were on earth, he should not be a priest, seeing that there are priests that offer gifts according to the law."* In the spiritual realm, He operated as a priest being fully God, but in the earthly realm, Jesus operated as the sacrifice and not a priest. Jesus was preparing them to be priests of the Lord here. He was preparing them for the "royal priesthood" (1

Pt. 2:9) and to minister in the Holy Spirit. Jesus' actions involve the transference of that priesthood in Heaven. Here God was changing the order from the Levitical priesthood to the Melchizedek priesthood.

Let me give you a little side note. Some say paying tithes is under the Levitical priesthood, but not under the priesthood of Melchizedek. Hebrews 7:1-8, *"For this Melchisedec, king of Salem, priest of the most high God, who met Abraham returning from the slaughter of the kings, and blessed him; To whom also Abraham gave a tenth part of all; first being by interpretation King of righteousness, and after that also King of Salem, which is, King of peace; Without father, without mother, without descent, having neither beginning of days, nor end of life; but made like unto the Son of God; abideth a priest continually. Now consider how great this man was, unto whom even the patriarch Abraham gave the tenth of the spoils. And verily they that are of the sons of Levi, who receive the office of the priesthood, have a commandment to take tithes of the people according to the law, that is, of their brethren, though they come out of the loins of Abraham: But he whose descent is not counted from them received tithes of Abraham, and blessed him that had the promises. And without all contradiction the less is blessed of the better. And here men that die receive tithes; but there he receiveth them, of whom it is witnessed that he liveth."* Under the Levitical priesthood, people gave tithes to men that eventually died, and God honored it. When you pay tithes now, you are giving back to Jesus who lives forever.

Let's go back to the subject of the foot washing. Exodus 30:17-21, *"And the Lord spake unto Moses, saying, Thou shalt also make a laver of brass, and his foot also of brass, to wash withal: and thou shalt put it between the tabernacle of the congregation and the altar, and thou shalt put water therein. For Aaron and his sons shall wash their hands and their feet thereat: When they go into the tabernacle of the congregation, they shall wash with water, that they die not; or when they come near to the altar to minister, to burn offering made by fire unto the Lord: So they shall wash their hands and their feet, that they die not: and it shall be a statute for ever to them, even to him and to his seed throughout their generations."*

Jesus was washing the disciples' feet for a royal priesthood. Such washing consecrated them for their sacred tasks ahead. Jesus was doing this for the disciples. He consecrated them for the ministry of reconciliation. John 13:9-10, *"Simon Peter saith unto him, Lord, not my feet only, but also my hands and my head. Jesus saith to him, He that is washed needeth not save to wash his feet, but is clean every whit: and ye are clean, but not all."* For weeks, I wrestled with why Jesus only washed their feet and not their hands too if He was consecrating them for service in the Holy Place to prepare them for the Holy Spirit. Then one morning, my wife, Connie, was reading John 13 to me and it came to me. As she was reading these verses John 13:12-17, *"So after he had washed their feet, and had taken his garments, and was set down again, he said unto them, Know ye what I have done to you? Ye call me Master and Lord: and ye say well; for so I am. If I then, your Lord and Master, have washed your feet; ye also ought to wash one another's feet. For I have given you an example, that ye should do as I have done to you. Verily, verily, I say unto you, The servant is not greater than his lord; neither he that is sent greater than he that sent him. If ye know these things, happy are ye if ye do them."*

Jesus gave them an example. I was thinking about what He had done, and how He washed their feet but not their hands. When she read verse 14, it came to me. If you wash someone else's feet, what part of you is cleansed? "It is your hands." I did masonry work for a living and sometimes the cracks in my hands were hard to get clean. One time, God spoke to us to wash the whole congregation's feet at Cornerstone Covenant Church. Connie washed the ladies' feet and I washed the gentlemen's feet. I looked at my hands afterwards, they were cleaner than when I washed them for myself.

Why did Jesus respond this way to Peter when he asked Jesus to wash his hands and head? Exodus 29:4 reads, *"And Aaron and his sons thou shalt bring unto the door of the tabernacle of the congregation, and shalt wash them with water."* An initiatory bath was valid for life. There is no evidence that it must be repeated. Your initial coming to the Lord is like a bath in which you are washed all over; completely from head to toe, inside and out. Jesus was saying, when you first come to me, you were bathed. I washed away all the guilt and sin of your entire life. But as you walk through life, Jesus knew your feet would be defiled during your walk and you would need to be washed again.

This cleansing will determine if we have a part with Him. There are those today who refuse to let Jesus wash their feet (your feet signify where you walk and what you are doing). When you refuse to let Jesus wash your feet, you lose that partnership with the Lord. God is no longer working with you. The Father has a business and Jesus and the Father want you to be part of that family business. You have the opportunity to become heirs and joint heirs with Christ, He offers you a partnership in the family business. Mark 16:20 says, *"And they went forth, and preached every where,* **the Lord working with them***, and confirming the word with signs following. Amen."* I don't know about you, but I need the Lord working with me.

JESUS PROPHESIES JUDAS' BETRAYAL

Then Jesus made the shell-shocking announcement that one of His trusted twelve disciples would betray Him, *"I speak not of you all: I know whom I have chosen: but that the scripture may be fulfilled, He that eateth bread with me hath lifted up his heel against me. Now I tell you before it come, that, when it is come to pass, ye may believe that I am he. Verily, verily, I say unto you, He that receiveth whomsoever I send receiveth me; and he that receiveth me receiveth him that sent me. When Jesus had thus said, he was troubled in spirit, and testified, and said,* **Verily, verily, I say unto you, that one of you shall betray me***. Then the disciples looked one on another, doubting of whom he spake. Now there was leaning on Jesus' bosom one of his disciples, whom Jesus loved. Simon Peter therefore beckoned to him, that he should ask who it should be of whom he spake. He then lying on Jesus' breast saith unto him, Lord, who is it? Jesus answered, He it is, to whom I shall give a sop, when I have dipped it. And when he had dipped the sop, he gave it to Judas Iscariot, the son of Simon. And after the sop Satan entered into him. Then said Jesus unto him, That thou doest, do quickly. Now no man at the table knew for what intent he spake this unto him. For some of them thought, because Judas had the bag, that Jesus had said unto him, Buy those things that we have need of against the feast; or, that he should give something to the poor. He then having received the sop went immediately out: and it was night. Therefore, when he was gone out, Jesus said, Now is the*

THE LAST SUPPER (John 13)

Son of man glorified, and God is glorified in him. If God be glorified in him, God shall also glorify him in himself, and shall straightway glorify him. Little children, yet a little while I am with you. Ye shall seek me: and as I said unto the Jews, Whither I go, ye cannot come; so now I say to you. A new commandment I give unto you, That ye love one another; as I have loved you, that ye also love one another. By this shall all men know that ye are my disciples, if ye have love one to another. Simon Peter said unto him, Lord, whither goest thou? Jesus answered him, Whither I go, thou canst not follow me now; but thou shalt follow me afterwards. Peter said unto him, Lord, why cannot I follow thee now? I will lay down my life for thy sake. Jesus answered him, Wilt thou lay down thy life for my sake? Verily, Verily, I say unto thee, The cock shall not crow, till thou hast denied me thrice" (John 13:18-38).

Now, the disciples looked at each other and wondered who the traitor was. Peter told John to ask Jesus who would betray Him. Jesus did not expose Judas openly even though He knew he was a thief from the beginning. Jesus still loved him. Jesus answered John, *"He it is, to whom I shall give a sop, when I have dipped it. And when he had dipped the sop,* **he gave it to Judas Iscariot***, the son of Simon"* (John 13:26). What is the significance of Jesus giving Judas a morsel of bread to identify Him as the one who would betray Him? Why didn't He just simply point him out? They were all asking who it was. That was done specifically to fulfill Psalms 41:9—*"Yea, mine own familiar friend, in whom I trusted, which did eat of my bread,* **hath lifted up his heel against me***."*

To lift up your heel against someone means to walk away from them. However, Jesus was still showing grace and mercy toward Judas. (The other disciples were totally unaware of what Judas was about to do). Jesus knew Judas' intentions all along. In verse 2, the devil had put the idea in his heart, but now Satan himself entered into Judas. John 13:28-30 reveals how oblivious the other disciples were of Judas' plans—*"Now **no man at the table knew for what intent he spake this unto him**. For some of them thought, because Judas had the bag, that Jesus had said unto him, Buy those things that we have need of against the feast; or, that he should give something to the poor. He then having received the sop went immediately out: and it was night."* Jesus had just told Judas, *"What you are going to do, do it quickly."* which he understood, but the others did not. To dip your bread in the sop and give it to someone was a sign of true friendship.

I want you to see the difference in Judas' and Peter's words. *"Then Judas, which betrayed him, answered and said, **MASTER, is it I**? He said unto him, Thou hast said"* (Matthew 26:25). Judas only saw Jesus as a "master" (Rabbi), or a teacher, while Peter saw Him as Lord (Messiah). Immediately when Judas went out, it was night (John 13:30). It was the darkest hour of the night. I am amazed at Jesus calling a traitor, His "friend." Matthew 26:48-50 informs us, *"Now he that betrayed him gave them a sign, saying, Whomsoever I shall kiss, that same is he: hold him fast. And forthwith he came to Jesus, and said, Hail, master; and kissed him. And Jesus said unto him, **Friend**, wherefore art thou come? Then came they, and laid hands on Jesus and took him"*

The only thing new in this commandment was the part "as I have loved you."

Lastly, let's look closer at John 13:34-35, *"A new commandment I give unto you, That ye love one another; as*

I have loved you, that ye also love one another. By this shall all men know that ye are my disciples, if ye have love one to another." Jesus gave a "new commandment." The only thing new in this commandment was the part "as I have loved you." In Leviticus 19:18, God told the Israelites, *"Thou shalt not avenge, nor bear any grudge against the children of thy people, but thou shalt **love thy neighbour as thyself**: I am the Lord."* At this supper, Jesus changed the motive of love from "as thyself" to "as I have loved you." To love one's neighbor as one's self was familiar among the Jews. But Jesus was showing a new measure of love greater than all love that had ever been shown. Jesus not only loved His neighbor as Himself, but He loved them more than Himself.

As Christ just showed them all His agape love, you should go and love freely even those who walk away and betray you. Christ had loved them not in word only, but also in deed and in truth (1 John 3:8). Peter later instructed us to *"Love one another with a pure heart fervently"* (1 Pt. 1:22), and Paul added, *"By love, serve one another"* (Gal. 5:13). There is an old quote, "wishes from dying lips are sacred." Up to this point, the only reason these disciples had stayed together was that Jesus was in their midst. Jesus was preparing them for His absence, which we will address later.

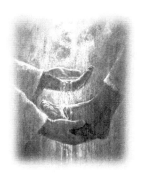

CHAPTER 2

THE MARRIAGE COVENANT
(John 14)

We just concluded the Last Supper in the upper room the night before Jesus' crucifixion in John 13. As previously noted, John 13-17 is commonly known as the "Upper Room Discourse." In chapter 13, Jesus revealed to His disciples that He was going to die. John chapters 14-17 are also commonly known as the "Farewell Discourse," which was given immediately after the conclusion of the Last Supper. Jesus was in anguish for all His disciples whom He loved— *"Now before the feast of the passover, when Jesus knew that his hour was come that he should depart out of this world unto the Father, **having loved his own** which were in the world, **he loved them** unto the end"* (John 13:1). Before the day was over, He would leave them and His words were spoken, above all, to bring comfort to them.

During this conversation, Jesus no longer called His disciples servants but "friends"—*"Henceforth I call you not servants; for the servant knoweth not what his lord doeth: but **I have called you friends**; for all things that I have heard of my Father I have made known unto you"* (John 15:15). Jesus promised not to leave them as orphans to go through life in their own strength—*"I will not leave you*

comfortless*: I will come to you"* (John 14:18). The Greek word translated "comfortless" is *orphanos* from which we derive the word "orphan." Jesus was reassuring the disciples that He would not leave them alone. Through the Spirit, He would continue to be with them. *"Verily, verily, I say unto you, He that believeth on me, the works that I do shall he do also; and greater works than these shall he do; because I go unto my Father"* (John 14:12). The eleven disciples were getting worried by this time. They had been expecting a coronation of Jesus as King of kings. They had expected it to be as the prophets foretold, but first Jesus had to come as a suffering Savior. This was prophesied in great detail in Isaiah 53 and Psalms 22. Recently, Jesus had been talking more about His death and rising back to life again after three days. This was not part of the disciples' plans. In just a few hours, all their plans would be changed forever. Jesus, trying to calm and prepare them, began talking of the future beyond the cross.

Jesus started with these words of comfort, *"Let not your heart be troubled: ye believe in God, believe also in me. In my Father's house are many mansions: if it were not so, I would have told you. I go to prepare a place for you. And if I go and prepare a place for you, I will come again, and receive you unto myself; that where I am, there ye may be also"* (John 14:1-3). Ask yourself what is the Father's House? Jesus said plainly that in His Father's house, there were many "mansions." If it had not been true, He said, He would have told us. The Greek word translated "mansions" means "a room, place of staying, an abode, or a chamber." So, in the Father's house there are a number of rooms or chambers. But what is the Father's house? What does the Bible declare the Father's house to be? When inside the Temple, Jesus said to the merchants who were selling oxen, doves, and cattle, and the money-changers, *"Take these things hence; make not my **Father's house** an house of merchandise"* (John 2:16). The Temple at Jerusalem was an earthly type of the Father's house in heaven. Luke's version states, *"And he went into the temple, and began to cast out them that sold therein, and them that bought; Saying unto them, It is written, **My house is the house of prayer**: but ye have made it a den of thieves"* (Luke 19:45-46). Jesus was quoting the Prophet Isaiah when he said of the Temple, "My house is a house of prayer." *"Even them will I bring to my holy mountain, and make them joyful in my house of prayer: their burnt offerings and their sacrifices shall be accepted upon mine altar; for **mine house shall be called an house of prayer** for all people"* (Isaiah 56:7). So, the Temple at Jerusalem in Christ's day was a type of the Father's house in heaven.

JEWISH WEDDING CUSTOMS

The fourteenth chapter of John is a promise of betrothal! Let's look at the customs of the Jewish wedding in Bible times. Without the understanding of their customs, we won't be able to understand the fullness of this amazing promise. The first major step in the Jewish marriage began with the establishment of a marriage covenant. The bridegroom took the initiative by traveling from his father's house to the prospective bride's home. When he arrived, he would negotiate with her father the price (known as a dowry) to become married to her. Once the bridegroom had paid the agreed price, the marriage covenant was

> *The first major step in the Jewish marriage began with the establishment of a marriage covenant.*

established, and the couple were regarded to be husband and wife. The price for Jesus to become our bridegroom was His precious blood. *"Forasmuch as ye know that ye were not **redeemed** with corruptible things, as silver and gold, from your vain conversation received by tradition from your fathers; But with **the precious blood of Christ**, as of a lamb without blemish and without spot"* (1 Peter 1:18). We, the Bride of Christ, have been purchased and now await the marriage supper. When we observe communion, we should remember Jesus didn't purchase our sins, but purchased us from our sins. From this point, the bride is considered consecrated or set aside exclusively for her bridegroom. As a symbol to mark and seal this covenant, the bride and groom would drink from a cup of wine. This was beautifully symbolized when Jesus shared the cup of wine with His disciples at the Last Supper.

Jesus gave them a new commandment as His bride. *"A **new commandment** I give unto you, That ye **love one another**; as I have loved you, that ye also love one another. By this shall all men know that ye are my disciples, if ye have love one to another"* After the marriage covenant had been established, the groom would return to his father's house. Jesus indicated this when He said, *"I go to prepare a place for you"* (John 14:2). The groom would begin preparing living accommodations at his father's house. As he was working at his father's house, he would often send gifts to his bride to let her know he had not forgotten her in his absence. When the dwelling place was done, the groom would come to take the bride to live with him. This usually took place at night. He would take his groomsmen and form a torch-light procession to the bride's home. She expected her groom to come for her, but she didn't know the exact time of his arrival. His arrival would be preceded by a shout. After the groom received her and all her bridesmaids, they would return to his father's house. (Jesus alluded to this Jewish wedding custom in His Parable of the Ten Virgins—Matthew 25:1-13).

Once they arrived, the wedding guests would already be assembled. Not long after their arrival, they would be escorted to the bridal chamber (*huppah*). The bride would remain veiled so that no one could see her face. While everyone waited outside, the bride and groom would enter the bridal chamber by themselves to consummate their marriage by physical intimacy. After the marriage was consummated, the groom would make the big announcement to those waiting outside the wedding chamber and the "Marriage Supper" (feast, what we know as a reception) would begin. John the Baptist said, *"He that hath the bride is the bridegroom: but the friend of the bridegroom, which standeth and heareth him, rejoiceth greatly because of the bridegroom's voice: this my joy therefore is fulfilled"* (John 3:29).

John the Revelator saw the Marriage Supper of the Lamb vividly in a vision, *"Let us be glad and rejoice, and give honour to him: for* **the marriage of the Lamb is come***, and his wife hath made herself ready. And to her was granted that she should be arrayed in fine linen, clean and white: for the fine linen is the righteousness of saints. And he saith unto me, Write, Blessed are they which are called unto* **the marriage supper of the Lamb***. And he saith unto me, These are the true sayings of God"* (Revelation 19:7-9). The Marriage Supper will start when the "Feast of Tabernacles" begins. During the seven days, the bride would remain hidden until the eighth day known as "Simchat Torah." This day marks a new beginning or, as I believe, it is a type or foreshadowing of the millennial reign with Christ.

DANCING WITH THE TORAH

"Simchat Torah" (rejoicing with the Torah) is a joyous celebration that celebrates the Jewish love of the Torah (the Law or Word of God). They will, even to this day, kiss the Torah as if marrying themselves to it. I have been in Jerusalem and celebrated this joyful event with the Jewish people. It is a day of great celebration all over Jerusalem. One year, I went to Independence Park where tens of thousands of Jews were celebrating. They had a fence set up that only Jews could go through and all Gentiles had to stay outside the gate. The Israeli Army was on guard. A Jewish friend of mine was inside. She asked me if I wanted to come inside the gate. I said "Yes." So, she said go get in line and as you come to the guards, I will distract them, and you can just come in. I did as she told me. Outside the gate was considered the "Outer Court." I went into what they considered the "Holy Place." I rejoiced with tears of joy. I kept dancing closer and closer to the front of the crowd. When I got to the front, there was a rock wall and the soldiers were spaced about four feet apart along the wall. Over that wall was a platform where the Rabbis and the men who had purchased a copy of the Torah handwritten by a scribe were standing. Their sons and other males were with them. The one who purchased the Torah would be considered a groom and his sons and other men would be considered the groomsmen. The

> *"Simchat Torah" (rejoicing with the Torah) is a joyous celebration that celebrates the Jewish love of the Torah.*

Torah was considered the "bride." They would dance with it and kiss the Torah (Word of God).

I couldn't take it any longer, so I made my way next to the wall between two soldiers. When they both looked away, I went over the wall. I joined the men dancing in a circle. I became so tired, so I sat down on a rock to rest a minute. A Jew from New York sat down beside me and said, "We all know you are not a Jew, but we can see your love for the Torah." I thanked him because they had preserved the Torah for us. Even Paul referred to this, *"What advantage then hath the Jew? or what profit is there of circumcision? Much every way: chiefly, because that **unto them were committed the oracles of God**."* (Romans 3:1-2). I expressed to the man how I was a Christian and loved the Torah. He asked me if I wanted to dance with one of the Torahs. I immediately said "YES!" There was a stage where the new Torahs (brides) were, which was considered a type of the Ark of the Covenant. They would dance with the Torah on the stage as though they were dancing in the Holy of Holies with their "bride" before the Ark (presence of the Lord). Zephaniah 3:17 described it this way, *"The Lord thy God in the midst of thee is mighty; he will save, he will rejoice over thee with joy; he will rest in his love, he will joy over thee with singing."* In this verse, the phrase "rejoice over thee" literally means "to dance, skip, leap, and spin around in joy over us." Simchat Torah is celebrated by taking all the Torah scrolls out of the "ark" (a fancy, beautiful container) in the synagogue and spending the evening dancing, singing, and rejoicing. This event has forever changed me and established my absolute love for God's Word.

In light of the promises Jesus made in John 14, let's look at Ephesians 5:22-23, *"Wives, submit yourselves unto your own husbands, as unto the Lord. For the husband is the head of the wife, even as Christ is the head of the church: and he is the saviour of the body."* Notice verse 23 tells us we are His body. Paul wrote about the Last Supper in 1 Corinthians 11:25, *"After the same manner also he took the cup, when he had supped, saying, This cup is the new testament in my blood: this do ye, as oft as ye drink it, in remembrance of me."* In doing this, we are remembering the covenant He established (the New Covenant) through the shedding of His blood on the cross. His blood is the price He paid to redeem and ransom His bride—*"What? Know ye not that your body is the temple of the Holy Ghost which is in you, which ye have of God, and* **ye are not your own**? **For ye are bought with a price**" (1 Corinthians 6:19-20). This verse tells us we are not our own. We like the Jewish bride, were sanctified, and set apart for our groom and for Him alone.

Paul alluded to this sanctification process in Ephesians 5:25-27, *"Husbands, love your wives, even as Christ also loved the church, and gave himself for it;* **That he might sanctify and cleanse it with the washing of water by the word**, *That he might present it to himself a glorious church, not having spot, or wrinkle, or any such thing; but that it should be holy and without blemish."* The writer of Hebrews agreed, *"By the which will we are* **sanctified** *through the offering of the body of Jesus Christ once for all"* (Hebrews 10:10). *"Wherefore Jesus also, that he might sanctify the people with his own blood, suffered without the gate"* (Hebrews 13:12). Jesus drank the cup at the beginning of the marriage covenant (Last Supper), but He won't drink it again until we are at the Father's house (Matthew 26:29). However, the bride will drink this cup often in remembrance of the groom (1 Corinthians 11:25

above). The disciples understood this analogy and Paul used the marriage metaphor to describe Christ and the church, *"For I am jealous over you with godly jealousy: for **I have espoused you to one husband, that I may present you as a chaste virgin to Christ**. But I fear, lest by any means, as the serpent beguiled Eve through his subtilty, so your minds should be corrupted from the simplicity that is in Christ"* (2 Corinthians 11:2-3). If you have been unfaithful to Him as His bride, confess it to Him. *"If we suffer, we shall also reign with him: if we deny him, he also will deny us: If we believe not, **yet he abideth faithful**: he cannot deny himself"* (2 Timothy 2:12-13). Even when we falter, He will always be faithful.

Let's return to my story about dancing with the Torah. When I said, "YES, I would love to dance with the Torah," the man from New York took me to the stage and the Rabbi stopped us. He said, "This man cannot dance with the Torah because he is not Jewish!" My friend immediately replied, "He is Jewish in his heart." By this time tears were flowing from my eyes. The Rabbi responded by saying, "He doesn't have a Kippah (skull cap) on." My friend answered the Rabbi back by taking his Kippah off and placing it on my head. Paul explained, *"For he is not a Jew, which is one outwardly; neither is that circumcision, which is outward in the flesh: **He is a Jew, which is one inwardly**; and circumcision is that of the heart, in the spirit, and not in the letter; whose praise is not of men, but of God"*

(Roman 2:28-29). My tears started flowing like a river. He looked at the Rabbi and said, "I paid $60,000 to have that Torah made" (it was a new Torah handwritten by a scribe on sheep skin). My friend went on to say, "This man is my family now and he will dance with the Torah." The Rabbi reluctantly moved out of the way and let us pass. My dear friend picked up a Torah and handed it to me. I embraced that Torah and begin to dance with it around the stage. I held it as tight as I could, if you drop the Torah and it touches the ground, they will bury it. Instead of rejoicing, they would be weeping over the dropped Torah. As I began to dance, my friend and his family all joined in with me celebrating my being married to the Torah. You might ask "Why do you love the Torah so much?" Because it is the Word and promise of God!

ISAAC AND REBEKAH— A TYPE OF CHRIST AND THE CHURCH

In the next chapter we will talk about "greater works," but first, look with me at John 14:15-18, *"If ye love me, keep my commandments. And I will pray the Father, and he shall give you another Comforter, that he may abide with you for ever; Even the Spirit of truth; whom the world cannot receive, because it seeth him not, neither knoweth him: but ye know him; for he dwelleth with you, and shall be in you. I will not leave you comfortless: I will come to you."*

The bride was usually chosen by the father of the bridegroom. The father would send his trusted servant, known as the "agent," to search for the bride. This custom was followed when Abraham selected a bride for his son Isaac, *"And Abraham was old, and well stricken in age: and the Lord had blessed Abraham in all thing. And* **Abraham said unto his eldest servant of his house**, *that ruled over all that he had, Put, I pray thee, thy hand under my thigh: And I will make thee swear by the Lord, the God of heaven, and the God of the earth, that thou shalt not take a wife unto my son of the daughters of the Canaanites, among whom I dwell: But thou shalt go unto my country, and to my kindred, and* **take a wife unto my son Isaac**" (Genesis 24:1-4).

In this passage, Abraham (a type of God the Father) wanted to secure a bride for Isaac (a type of Jesus, the Messiah) and sent his servant Eliezer (a type of the Holy Spirit) to perform this task. It is the role of the Holy Spirit to convict the world of sin and lead them to God as Jesus described in John 16:7-8, *"Nevertheless I tell you the truth; It is expedient for you that I go away: for if I go not away, the Comforter will not come unto you; but if I depart, I will send him unto you. And when he is come,* **he will reprove the world of sin**, *and of righteousness, and of judgment."*

Just as the bride was usually chosen by the father of the groom, so the believers in the Messiah are chosen by God. Jesus said, *"Ye have not chosen me, but* **I have chosen you**, *and ordained you, that ye should go and bring forth fruit, and that your fruit should remain: that whatsoever ye shall ask of the Father in my name, he may give it you"* (John 15:16). In the Jewish custom, the bridegroom chose the bride and lavished his love upon her, and she returned his love. This can be seen in Ephesians 5:25,

> *Just as the bride was usually chosen by the father of the groom, so the believers in the Messiah are chosen by God.*

"Husbands, love your wives, even as Christ also loved the church, and gave himself for it."

Notice that Rebekah consented to marry Isaac even before she ever met him. Today, the believers in the Messiah consent to become the bride of Christ even though we have never physically seen Him. 1 Peter 1:8 expresses this truth, **"Whom having not seen, ye love;** *in whom, though now ye see him not, yet believing, ye rejoice with joy unspeakable and full of glory."* A covenant contract was drawn up stating the bride's price or dowry. The blood of Jesus was the promise of our heavenly groom and established the rights of the bride. The groom promised to work for her, to honor her, support her, and maintain her in truth. He provided food, clothing, and necessities, and they lived together as husband and wife. This contract was the unchangeable right of the bride. The contract must be executed and signed prior to the wedding ceremony. The Word of God is the believer's contract. All the promises that God provided for the believers in Christ are legally ours. 2 Corinthians 1:20 declares, *"For all the promises of God in him are yea, and in him Amen, unto the glory of God by us."* By saying "yea," you are saying "yes" or "I do" to the Lord Jesus. When you say "AMEN," it is as though you are signing the contract. Jesus' bride will be stunningly beautiful.

The Apostle John, the beloved, caught a glimpse of her beauty which is beyond description when he saw the revelation of the "bride, the Lamb's wife." *"And there came unto me one of the seven angels which had the seven vials full of the seven last plagues, and talked with me, saying, Come hither, I will shew thee* **the bride, the Lamb's wife***"* (Revelation 21:9). This honor to be the bride and a joint-heir with Christ is opened to all the ransomed church of

God! Can you hear the call of the Spirit? The Spirit is calling you to become the Bride of Christ. The Holy Spirit, typified by Eliezer, brings gifts from the Bridegroom and His Father. *"And it came to pass, that, when Abraham's servant heard their words, he worshipped the Lord, bowing himself to the earth. And the servant brought forth jewels of silver, and jewels of gold, and raiment, and gave them to Rebekah: he gave also to her brother and to her mother precious things"* (Genesis 24:52-53). Just as Abraham through Eliezer gave gifts to Rebekah, the bride of Isaac, even so God through the Holy Spirit has given gifts to the church, the bride of Christ (1 Corinthians 12:8-10, Ephesians 4:7-13).

I want you to look at the relationship between the Holy Spirit and the bride. We see it in this verse—*"And **the Spirit and the bride** say, Come. And let him that heareth say, Come. And let him that is athirst come. And whosoever will, let him take the water of life freely"* (Revelation 22:17). The eternal purpose of the Holy Spirit and His gifts is to bring us home to live with Jesus Christ our bridegroom as His eternal, spotless bride. Eliezer's name means "mighty, divine helper." He is a fitting type of the Holy Spirit. Oddly, Eliezer's name is never mentioned in the Genesis 24 as he seeks out Isaac's bride. He is only mentioned in Genesis 15:2 as the steward of Abraham's household. Jesus promised to send the Holy Spirit, *"But the Comforter, which is the Holy Ghost, whom the Father will send in my name, he shall teach you all things, and bring all things to your remembrance, whatsoever I have said unto you"* (John 14:26). The Holy Spirit is our Comforter, which also means an Advocate, Defender, or Helper. He is an advocate between us and the Father. He is the marriage covenant or contract keeper. He is a helper to assist us and remind us to keep that contract. He helps us obey the Commandments. Without the Holy Spirit, none of us can consistently keep the Commandments. We can't even live a victorious, Christian life without His assistance.

Everything the Holy Spirit does is related to His purpose stated in John 14:26—*"But the Comforter, which is the Holy Ghost, whom the Father will send in my name, he shall **teach you all things, and bring all things to your remembrance**, whatsoever I have said unto you."* He will bring us home to our bridegroom, Jesus, as a prepared bride, who has made herself ready. He is keeping us on track with that mission! Yes, He is our Guide, our Comforter, and our Strength in the time of need. But he uses every deliverance, every touch, every manifestation of Himself to prepare us as the bride. However, the Holy Spirit hasn't come just to give gifts to the world. No, His every gift has a purpose behind it. If He enables you to prophesy, that prophecy has this purpose: to glorify Christ and to make the world and His church fall in love with Him! Every time someone is healed, the Holy Spirit is saying, "That's your Jesus! Isn't He wonderful?" He is healing you and you're just seeing the manifestation of who He is.

Paul called the Holy Spirit the "earnest" (just a down payment) of our total inheritance in Christ! *"Ye were sealed with that holy Spirit of promise, Which is **the earnest of our inheritance** until the redemption of the purchased possession, unto the praise of his glory"* (Ephesians 1:14). We are that "purchased possession"—His blood-bought bride. All the gifts of the Holy Spirit are our gifts from our bridegroom and His Father. When giving these gifts, the Holy Spirit is saying, "Do you love Jesus? Look at what He's done for you!" Everything the Holy Spirit does points to Jesus, for the Spirit does not speak of Himself. *"Howbeit* *when he, the Spirit of truth, is come, he will guide you into all truth: for **he shall not speak of himself**; but whatsoever he shall hear, that shall he speak: and he will shew you things to come"* (John 16:13). We will refer to and elaborate on these concepts later. I pray you now have a better understanding of the marriage covenant our Lord has given those who accept His proposal. The Creator of the universe is in love with YOU—His eternal bride!

CHAPTER 3

JESUS—THE TRUE VINE
(John 15)

For a moment, let's look at John 14:31, *"But that the world may know that I love the Father; and as the Father gave me commandment, even so I do. Arise, let us go hence."* At this time, Jesus and His disciples rose from the Passover supper and went to the Mount of Olives. The remainder of this Discourse, recorded in John 15-17, was delivered on the way to or in the Garden of Gethsemane. It was probably close to midnight. Because it was Passover, the moon was full as they walked in the night and communed with one another. In this verse, Jesus told His disciples that it was important to Him that the world knew that He died not for His own sins, but for their sins. Furthermore, He loved the Father and was obedient to everything He commanded Him to do. *"And being found in fashion as a man, he humbled himself, and **became obedient unto death**, even the death of the cross"* (Philippians 2:8).

In John 15:1-3, Jesus used an agricultural analogy, *"I am **the true vine**, and my Father is the husbandman. Every branch in me that beareth not fruit he taketh away: and every branch that beareth fruit, he purgeth it, that it may bring forth more fruit. Now ye are clean through the word which I have spoken unto you."* Jesus revealed

Himself as the True Vine. The disciples were familiar with the symbolism of a vine. God had repeatedly used a vine as a symbol of His people. *"Thou hast brought **a vine** out of Egypt: thou hast cast out the heathen, and planted it. Thou preparedst room before it, and didst cause it to take deep root, and it filled the land"* (Psalms 80:8-9). The Prophet Jeremiah wrote, *"Yet I had planted thee **a noble vine**, wholly a right seed: how then art thou turned into the degenerate plant of a strange vine unto me?"* (Jeremiah 2:21). Hosea 10:1 makes this comparison, *"Israel is **an empty vine**, he bringeth forth fruit unto himself: according to the multitude of his fruit he hath increased the altars; according to the goodness of his land they have made goodly images."*

The vine was also recognized as a symbol of the Messiah. Israel was just a symbol, but Jesus is the True Vine. We must abide in Him if we are going to produce the fruit of the Spirit Paul spoke about in Galatians 5:22-23, *"But the **fruit of the Spirit** is love, joy, peace, longsuffering, gentleness, goodness, faith, Meekness, temperance: against such there is no law."* Jesus said, *"My father is the **husbandman**"* which means the vine dresser or the gardener. A vineyard must have a gardener or farmer to plant it, water it, and watch over it. Jesus was and is the vine of His Father's planting. He only sought the will of His Father in all He said and did. He became a man to show us what we (His creation) ought to be toward our Creator. Jesus not only took our place on the cross but, from His birth on, His life on earth was our example of how we should live in this present world. Christ lived the life of a man exactly as we should live ours. He is our ultimate role model.

In the Old Testament, God was presented many times as the Husbandman. My favorite example is Isaiah 27:2-6, *"In that day sing ye unto her, **A vineyard of red wine. I the Lord do keep it**; I will water it every moment: lest any hurt it, I will keep it night and day. Fury is not in me: who would set the briers and thorns against me in battle? I would go through them, I would burn them together. Or let him take hold of my strength, that he may make peace with me; and he shall make peace with me. He shall cause them that come of Jacob to take root: Israel shall blossom and bud, and fill the face of the world with fruit."* A vineyard of red wine could be symbolic of Christ's blood. The Lord will always keep it night and day and let no one hurt it. What a promise of divine protection! He also promised to remove the briers and the thorns from our life which choke the life from the vine. I especially love verse 6, *"Israel shall blossom and bud, and fill the face of the world with fruit."* What a great Husbandman and caretaker our heavenly Father is!

Notice John 15:2 again, *"Every **branch** in me that beareth not fruit he taketh away: and every branch that beareth fruit, he purgeth it, that it may bring forth more fruit."* Christ compared His disciples to branches and told them to stay connected to Him. Read the first part again, *"Every branch in me that beareth not fruit, He taketh away."* In Greek, the word for "taketh away" is also translated "lifts up." The Father "lifts up" the branches off the ground as was common with vine branches in those days and still is today. The Psalmist described how God lifts up His people in the following passages: *"The Lord upholdeth all that fall, and **raiseth up** all those that be bowed down"* (Psalms 145:14). *"The Lord openeth the eyes of the blind: **the Lord raiseth them that are bowed down**: the Lord loveth the righteous"* (Psalms 146:8). *"I will extol thee, O Lord; for **thou hast lifted me up**, and hast not made my foes to rejoice over me. O Lord my God, I cried unto thee, and thou hast healed me. O Lord, thou hast brought up my soul from the grave: thou hast kept me alive, that I should not go down to the pit" (Psalms 30:1-3). He lifts us up when we are down so we can get more sun (Son) and bear more fruit.

GOD'S PRUNING PROCESS

As stated in John 15:2, *"He **purgeth it**, that it may bring forth more fruit."* The Father "purges" or "prunes" the branches, which is also translated in other places as the word "cleanse." The Father is not going to let us grow wildly on our own. Some people produce fruit and then don't want to submit any longer to anyone else. I have seen it many times in ministry. Someone said to me, "If you leave a grapevine to itself, it will produce unproductive growth that will sap the life out of the branches." So, in order to produce much more, we must be purged occasionally. After a season of fruit bearing, we all need a good pruning! I have seen it many times, when we are fruitful, there is a temptation that comes in thinking that we did it ourselves. If we forget our source, the True Vine, the life will be sapped out of what we are doing! If we get disconnected from the vine, our branch will wither and die. We must stay connected to Christ!

John 15:3, *"Now ye are **clean** through the Word, which I have spoken unto you."* The Greek word translated "clean" here is the adjective form of the verb "purgeth" used in John 15:2. To "purge" means to "cleanse" and, here in verse 3, it means to "clean." In the following days, the disciples would be pruned more than they could ever imagine. Many things they believed would be cut away (pruned) as they experienced great loss. In times of great trial, we try to rebuke the devil, when many times it is the Father pruning us. When you are pruned, you will feel the pain of loss. In this time of pruning, we might have the feeling of giving up or drawing back from the purpose of God in our life. Peter described the pruning process, *"Wherein ye greatly rejoice, though now for a season, if need be, ye are in heaviness through manifold temptations: That the **trial of your faith**, being much more precious than of gold that perisheth, though it be tried with fire, might be found unto praise and honour and glory at the appearing of Jesus Christ: Whom having not seen, ye love; in whom, though now ye see him not, yet believing, ye rejoice with joy unspeakable and full of glory: Receiving the end of your faith, even the salvation of your souls"* (1 Peter 1:6-9).

Sometimes the pruning seasons help us refocus on the Word. It is the Word which cleanses us—"That he might sanctify and cleanse it with the washing of water by the word" (Ephesians 5:26). The cleansing by the Word will yield more fruit. I like the use of the word "yield" because that is what we must do to be cleansed and produce more fruit! Notice how even creation yields to the will of the Creator, *"And God said, Let the earth bring forth grass, the herb **yielding seed**, and the fruit tree **yielding fruit** after his kind, whose seed is in itself, upon the earth: and it was so. And the earth brought forth grass, and herb yielding seed after his kind, and the tree yielding fruit, whose seed was in itself, after his kind: and God saw that it was good"* (Genesis 1:11-12). We must yield to the husbandman (our heavenly Father).

ABIDING IN CHRIST

Jesus continued His discourse in John 15:4-9, *"**Abide** in me, and I in you. As the branch cannot bear fruit of itself, except it **abide** in the vine; no more can ye, except ye **abide** in me. I am the vine, ye are the branches: He that **abideth** in me, and I in him, the same bringeth forth much fruit: for without me ye can do nothing. If a man **abide** not in me, he is cast forth as a branch, and is withered; and men gather them, and cast them into the fire, and they are burned. If ye **abide** in me, and my words **abide** in you, ye shall ask what ye will, and it shall be done unto you. Herein is my Father glorified, that ye bear much fruit; so shall ye be my disciples. As the Father hath loved me, so have I loved you: continue ye in my love."* Notice that "abiding" is a two-way street. It isn't only us abiding in Jesus, but He is also abiding in us. To "abide" means "to stay, to continue, to dwell or to remain." We must stay in constant fellowship with Him. Otherwise, as He said, *"Without Him we can do nothing."*

Song of Solomon 6:3 reads, *"I am my beloved's, and my beloved is mine: he feedeth among the lilies."* Remember, Jesus was laying out His terms of the Marriage Covenant. In John 15:7, it is made clear that abiding in Christ means abiding in His Word. The conditions for this powerful prayer are that we must abide in Jesus and His words must abide in us. "The branch cannot bear fruit of itself except it abide in the vine, no more can ye, except ye abide in me." The branches can't produce fruit unless they are connected to the vine. All the sap (life) that flows in the branch comes from the vine. The next three verses (John 15:5-7) are talking about the relationship between the vine and the branches. Look at John 14:23, *"Jesus answered and said unto him, If a man love me, he will keep my words: and my Father will love him, and we will come unto him, and make our abode with him."* It starts out with "If you love me, My Father will love you." The term "abode" denotes "habitation, abiding place," or simply put means "home."

The term "abode" denotes "habitation, abiding place," or simply put means "home."

Look at the verse before this, *"Judas saith unto him, not Iscariot, Lord, how is it that thou wilt manifest thyself unto us, and not unto the world?"* (John 14:22) One of the disciples asked what Jesus meant when he said, "He will manifest Himself to them." The word "abode," translated "home," is the same word as "mansions" used in John 14:2 referring to "dwelling places" or "rooms" in the Father's house. It is also the same word as "abide" used several times in John 15. Jesus was saying that He will take up residence in the hearts of His disciples! Paul echoed this concept in 1 Corinthians 3:16, *"Know ye not that **ye are the temple of God**, and that the Spirit of God **dwelleth in you**?"* Later, he wrote, *"And what agreement hath the temple of God with idols? for ye are the temple of the living God; as God hath said, **I will dwell in them**, and walk in them; and I will be their God, and they shall be my people"* (2 Corinthians 6:16). *"To whom God would make known what is the riches of the glory of this mystery among the Gentiles; which is **Christ in you**, the hope of glory"* (Colossians 1:27). Someone once said, "Christ in you is the Hope of Glory and you in Christ is the Glory!" Our purpose as the branches is to bring glory and honor to the Father. Our connection to Christ is evident by the fruit we bear—much fruit!

Jesus said in Matthew 7:16, *"Ye shall know them by their fruits. Do men gather grapes of thorns, or figs of thistles?"* I searched and found that there are vines in the grape family that do not produce fruit which are known as a wild grape. Cultivated grapes have both male (Christ) and female (the church) parts in them. Those vines will self-pollinate and produce fruit. But the wild grape vines have separate male and female plants. Many of our wild vines, like poison ivy, are in the family which will destroy a tree, breaking the branches by loading them down. They will steal the water the tree needs to survive. The wild vines will plunder the soil of vital nutrients and pull it to the ground. They will snap off the top to kill it once and for all. They can produce inedible seeds that fall to the ground and multiply. When you cut one of these vines, much water comes pouring out, water that the tree could be using.

This gives new meaning to "without Him I can do nothing." Without Jesus, we can't produce any fruit. We can't do it on our own. It is only through the marriage with Christ that any branch can bear fruit. Once that union with Christ is broken, the sap no longer flows to the branches. It is then impossible for that branch to produce fruit. It will wither and die. As Jesus explained in John 15:6-8, *"If a man abide not in me, he is cast forth as a branch, and is withered; and men gather them, and cast them into the fire, and they are burned. If ye abide in me, and my words abide in you, ye shall ask what ye will, and it shall be done unto you. Herein is my Father glorified, that ye bear much fruit; so shall ye be my disciples."*

STAY CONNECTED TO THE VINE

I can't emphasize enough that we must stay connected to the vine. If we, the branches, are broken from the vine, we will die spiritually, but the vine will still live.

Dead branches must be removed, they are a destructive influence. Insects are attracted to dead branches. If you don't remove them, they will spread into the live branches. Fungi can develop and easily spread from the dead branches. Removing the dead, infected branches will save the grapevine. Notice our husbandman gathers them up and casts them into the fire. If you just leave them laying around, you risk spreading the destruction to uninfected branches. Bitterness is a good example, *"Looking diligently lest any man fail of the grace of God; lest any **root of bitterness** springing up trouble you, and thereby many be defiled"* (Hebrews 12:15).

Look also at these verses, *"Now the works of the flesh are manifest, which are these; Adultery, fornication, uncleanness, lasciviousness, Idolatry, witchcraft, hatred, variance, emulations, wrath, strife, seditions, heresies, Envyings, murders, drunkenness, revellings, and such like: of the which I tell you before, as I have also told you in time past, that they which do such things shall not inherit the kingdom of God"* (Galatians 5:19-21). The works of the flesh are dead works that hinder our fruitfulness, *"For they that are after the flesh do mind the things of the flesh; but they that are after the Spirit the things of the Spirit. For to be carnally minded is death; but to be spiritually minded is life and peace"* (Romans 8:5-6). I want the Father to remove all these dead branches from my life so I can thrive and be fruitful.

Notice how Jesus connected "abiding" to answered prayer, *"If ye abide in me, and my words abide in you,* **ye shall ask what ye will**, **and it shall be done unto you**" (John 15:7). *"And whatsoever ye shall ask in my name, that will I do, that the Father may be glorified in the Son.* ***If ye shall ask any thing in my name**, **I will do it**"* (John

14:13-14). Abiding in Him is also Him abiding in us. Living in Him is Him living in us. Walking in Him is Him walking in us. If you abide in Jesus, you abide in His Words and if He abides in us, His Words abide in us. Then we can "ask what we will" and it will be done. I believe those branches that have this connection with the Vine will not ask anything amiss so the Word declares, "It shall be done." *"Herein is my Father glorified, that ye bear much fruit; so shall ye be my disciples"* (John 15:8). Our purpose in bearing fruit is to bring Glory to the Father. If we bear much fruit, we bring Glory to the One that takes care of us. Notice it says, "much fruit." If we don't yield to the cleansing process, we might yield some fruit, but not much fruit. But if we yield, we will bring forth much fruit. Branches that bear much fruit are not self-seeking, but their desire is to bring Honor and Glory to their heavenly Husbandman.

Jesus continued in John 15:9-12, *"As the Father hath loved me, so have I loved you: continue ye in my love. If ye keep my commandments, ye shall abide in my love; even as I have kept my Father's commandments, and abide in his love. These things have I spoken unto you, that my joy might remain in you, and that your joy might be full. This is my commandment, That ye love one another, as I have loved you."* Abiding in Him and Him in you is abiding in His love and His love in you. Again, as Song of Solomon 6:3 states, *"I am my beloved's, and my beloved is mine."* We must stay connected to the True Vine through His love. To abide in His love, we must keep His commandments out of the pure motive of love for Him. Your level of love is always proportional to your level of obedience—*"If ye love me, keep my commandments"* (John 14:15). What Jesus did and taught His disciples that evening was to keep His commandments out of love for Him and one another. In John 15:11 above, Jesus spoke these things, *"That my joy might remain in you, and that your joy might be full."* 3 John 1:4 says, *"I have no greater joy than to hear that my children walk in truth."* The Lord's joy is for us to walk in truth (His Words). The Apostle John was expressing the same joy. Then Jesus made a interesting statement, *"Verily, verily, I say unto you, He that believeth on me, the works that I do shall he do also; and* **greater works than these shall he do**; *because I go unto my Father"* (John 14:12).

As I am writing this, I am seeing something new about the use of the word "greater." The Apostle John said, "no greater joy," as he walked in truth and taught others to do so. Then the "greater works" happened. In the same way, Jesus had shown grace to His disciples and they walked in that grace and then extended that same grace they experienced to others (great grace). *"And with* **great power** *gave the apostles witness of the resurrection of the Lord Jesus: and* **great grace** *was upon them all"* (Acts 4:33). Ephesians 1:19 adds, *"And what is the* **exceeding greatness of His power** *to us-ward who believe, according to the working of his* **mighty power**.*"* Look at the use of the words "great" and "greatness" in these verses. When we receive "His works" and walk in "His works," then we extend those works to others and the greater shows up.

Again, Jesus repeated His **New Commandment** in John 13:34, *"A new commandment I give unto you, That ye* **love one another**; **as I have loved you**, *that ye also love one another."* Remember, the only thing new was it was no longer "as thyself," but He changed it to, "as I have loved you." Listen carefully, Jesus really cares about your love for one another and that you love one another with the same love that He has shown you. He showed us what that looks like in John 15:13, *"Greater love hath* no man than this, that a man lay down his life for his friends." Jesus, just a few hours later, demonstrated this greater love to them. In fact, He went beyond laying down His life for His friends and even laid down His life for His enemies. The Apostle John, who was known as the "Apostle of Love," repeated this principle in 1 John 3:14-16, "We know that we have passed from death unto life, because we love the brethren. He that loveth not his brother abideth in death. Whosoever hateth his brother is a murderer: and ye know that no murderer hath eternal life abiding in him. Hereby perceive we the love of God, because **he laid down his life for us**: and we ought to **lay down our lives for the brethren**."

> *Jesus really cares about your love for one another and that you love one another with the same love that He has shown you.*

The previous verse states, *"Marvel not, my brethren, if the world hate you"* (1 John 3:13). Jesus said something similar in John 15:18, *"If the world hate you, ye know that it hated me before it hated you."* The Apostle John wrote these epistles in his old age, but he was still teaching what Jesus had taught Him on the night He was betrayed. Jesus was betrayed just a few hours before He was crucified. *"Ye are my friends, if ye do whatsoever I command you. Henceforth I call you not servants; for the servant knoweth not what his lord doeth: but I have called you friends; for all things that I have heard of my Father I have made known unto you. Ye have not chosen me, but I have chosen you, and ordained you, that ye should go and bring forth fruit, and that your fruit should remain: that whatsoever ye shall ask of the Father in my name, he may give it you. These things I command you, that ye love one another"* (John 15:14-17). Jesus had just talked to them about the cross. He bought us with His own blood to prove that He has chosen and accepted us. The only fruit that will ever endure to eternal life is the fruit which grows out of the power of the cross. We are Christ's fruit because He died for us. We are His fruit-bearers if we are willing to take up our cross and die with Him. AMEN! Death to the flesh! As Paul wrote, *"Though our outward man perish, yet the inward man is renewed day by day"* (2 Corinthians 4:16).

What was Jesus talking about when He said, "You have not chosen me, but I have chosen you?" Why did He say, "You did not choose me?" He did not make them follow Him kicking and screaming. These men were not looking for a way to escape. John 1:37-41 records their initial encounter with Christ, *"And the two disciples heard him speak, and they followed Jesus. Then Jesus turned, and saw them following, and saith unto them, What seek ye? They said unto him, Rabbi, (which is to say, being interpreted, Master,) where dwellest thou? He saith unto them, Come and see. They came and saw where he dwelt, and abode with him that day: for it was about the tenth hour. One of the two which heard John speak, and followed him, was Andrew, Simon Peter's brother. He first findeth his own brother Simon, and saith unto him, We have found the Messias, which is, being interpreted, the Christ."*

Andrew followed Jesus after hearing Him speak without even being asked. Then he went and found his brother, Peter, and brought him to Jesus. So, what was Jesus actually saying here? I believe He was saying, "You being here is all my doing and so I take full responsibility for you." In Genesis 12:1-2, God told Abraham, *"Now the Lord had said unto Abram, Get thee out of thy country, and from thy kindred, and from thy father's house, unto a land that I will shew thee: And I will make of thee a great* nation, and I will bless thee, and make thy name great; and thou shalt be a blessing." Notice God said, "I will make of thee." God was taking responsibility for Abraham. Jesus told Peter, *"Come ye after me, and **I will make you to become** fishers of men"* (Mark 1:17). If we are anything at all, it is because Christ took responsibility by choosing us by grace. Paul knew this truth well, *"But by **the grace of God I am what I am**: and his grace which was bestowed upon me was not in vain; but I laboured more abundantly than they all: **yet not I, but the grace of God which was with me"*** (1 Corinthians 15:10).

Look again at John 15:5, *"I am the vine, ye are the branches: He that abideth in me, and I in him, the same bringeth forth much fruit: **for without me ye can do nothing**."* We have been chosen to bear fruit. You didn't produce the Vine, the Vine produced you. He ordained you or appointed you. What did He appoint you for? That you should go and bear fruit, and that the fruit should remain. The secret to being fruitful is "abiding." Some form of the word "abide" is mentioned ten times in this chapter. If we abide in Him, His Word, and His love, then His Word, and His love will abide in us. With this spiritual connection, our prayer life and ministries will be much more effective. Notice when Jesus said, "Go and bring forth fruit," that they would later go to the nations. They would take the fruit throughout the world and reap souls from the whole world. Remember Isaiah 27:6? *"He shall cause them that come of Jacob to take root: Israel shall blossom and bud, and **fill the face of the world with fruit**."* But, read this promise carefully, *"That your fruit should **remain**."* To "remain" means "to stay or abide." How does it abide? By feeding

> *"Israel shall blossom and bud, and fill the face of the world with fruit."*

them the fruit, but you must plant the seed. How do we plant the seed? By making disciples! Jesus gave the Great Commission in Matthew 28:19-20, *"Go ye therefore, and teach all nations, baptizing them in the name of Father, and of the Son, and the Holy Ghost. Teaching them to observe all things whatsoever I have commanded you: and, lo, I am with you always, even unto the end of the world. Amen."* If you make disciples, you leave something that will remain. Feed them the Word and plant the seed so they can reproduce the same fruit.

HATED BY THE WORLD

Jesus cautioned the disciples in John 15:18, *"If the world hate you, ye know that it hated me before it hated you."* In this verse and throughout the rest of this chapter, Jesus warned them of how much they would be hated. They would be persecuted and all of them would die as martyrs except for John. They tried to kill John by boiling him in oil, but he miraculously would not die at their hands. So, they banished him to the Isle of Patmos where he saw inspired visions and wrote the book of Revelation. Christians throughout history have been hated by the world, and millions have died as martyrs. We, living in America, may not comprehend this next statement, but more Christians have died as martyrs in the 20th and the beginning of the 21st centuries than all the previous centuries combined. See the example of Paul in Acts 9:4, *"And he fell to the earth, and heard a voice saying unto him, Saul, Saul, why persecutest thou me?"* Jesus considered the persecution of His saints as a direct attack on Him.

In Acts 1:8, Jesus promised, *"But ye shall receive power, after that the Holy Ghost is come upon you: and ye shall be **witnesses** unto me both in Jerusalem, and in* *all Judaea, and in Samaria, and unto the uttermost part of the earth."* The word "witnesses" is translated from the Greek word *martus* from which we get the English word "martyr." A "martyr," or in this case, a "witness," is "someone who suffers persecution and death for advocating and refusing to renounce Jesus Christ and His teaching." Spiritually, you become a martyr by dying to the deeds of the flesh. Paul wrote, *"For if ye live after the flesh, ye shall die: but if ye through the Spirit do mortify the deeds of the body, ye shall live"* (Romans 8:13). To "mortify" means to put to death.

Jesus quoted from Psalms in John 15:25, *"But this cometh to pass, that the word might be fulfilled that is written in their law,* **They hated me without a cause**.*"* This was a fulfillment of a specific prophecy in Psalms 69:4, *"***They that hate me without a cause*** are more than the hairs of mine head: they that would destroy me, being mine enemies wrongfully, are mighty: then I restored that which I took not away."* There is no cause or reason for the world to hate Jesus and there is no reason for them to hate us. They hate Jesus and us (His disciples) because their deeds are evil, and they love darkness rather than light. *"And this is the condemnation, that light is come into the world, and* **men loved darkness rather than light, because their deeds were evil***"* (John 3:19). They will hate you not because of what you have done, but because of the conviction of their own deeds.

Remember, they hated Jesus first before they hate you. *"If the world hate you, ye know that it hated me before it hated you ... If I had not done among them the works which none other man did, they had not had sin: but now have they both seen and hated both me and my Father"* (John 15:18, 24). Jesus did many supernatural works such as healing the sick, raising the dead, giving sight to the blind, causing the dumb to speak, the deaf to hear, the lame to walk, cleansing lepers, and casting out devils, which was proof and full demonstration that He came from God and was truly the Messiah. *"How God anointed Jesus of Nazareth with the Holy Ghost and with power: who* **went about doing good, and healing all that were oppressed of the devil**; *for God was with him"* (Acts 10:38). Notice the phrase "Which none other man did" in John 15:24. No one had ever given sight to one born blind. Look at John 9:1, 32, *"And as Jesus passed by, he saw a man which was blind from his birth ... Since the world began was it not heard that any man opened the eyes of one that was born blind."* Jesus performed astounding miracles that no one had ever done before.

Young boy named Austin who was born deaf and dumb, but the Lord healed him in a meeting in North Carolina.

Next, in John 15:24, Jesus said, *"they had not had sin."* The works had been done among them openly, visibly, and publicly. They saw His works and miracles yet rejected Him. For that reason, they were blind. *"Now have they both seen and hated both Me and My Father."* They saw the miracles which were done by Jesus. It was prophesied that the Messiah would do these things. They had seen and yet they still hated Him. They hated Him not for His works, but because He revealed the evil in their hearts. The priests hated Him because of jealousy. Proverbs 27:4 says, *"Wrath is cruel, and anger is outrageous; but* **who is**

able to stand before envy?" Mark 15:9-10 records, *"But Pilate answered them, saying, Will ye that I release unto you the King of the Jews? For he knew that* **the chief priests had delivered him for envy**.*"* Envy is why they crucified our Lord. Jesus was teaching them not to envy one another, but to love one another as He had loved them."

He concluded by speaking of the Comforter in John 15:26-27, *"But when the* **Comforter** *is come, whom I will send unto you from the Father, even the Spirit of truth, which proceedeth from the Father, he shall testify of me: And ye also shall bear witness, because ye have been with me from the beginning."* They were given the privilege to bear witness because they had been with him from the beginning of His public ministry. I believe here, in these last two verses, the Comforter (the Holy Spirit) and the disciples (apostles) were joined together to fulfill the Great Commission, *"And he said unto them, Go ye into all the world, and preach the gospel to every creature. He that believeth and is baptized shall be saved; but he that believeth not shall be damned. And these signs shall follow them that believe; In my name shall they cast out devils; they shall speak with new tongues; They shall take up serpents; and if they drink any deadly thing, it shall not hurt them; they shall lay hands on the sick, and they shall recover. So then after the Lord had spoken unto them, he was received up into heaven, and sat on the right hand of God. And they went forth, and preached every where, the Lord working with them, and confirming the word with signs following. Amen."* (Mark 16:15-20). The apostles taught and preached the Word while the Holy Spirit worked the signs and wonders.

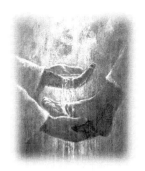

CHAPTER 4

WALKING AND TALKING WITH JESUS
(John 16)

In this chapter we will follow Jesus as He prepared the disciples for what was to come. In John 16:1-4, He predicted how they would be persecuted: *"These things have I spoken unto you, that ye should not be offended. They shall put you out of the synagogues: yea, the time cometh, that whosoever killeth you will think that he doeth God service. And these things will they do unto you, because they have not known the Father, nor me. But these things have I told you, that when the time shall come, ye may remember that I told you of them. And these things I said not unto you at the beginning, because I was with you."*

Jesus spoke to His disciples about being hated because He didn't want them to be offended or stumble and fall. He knew they would be forced out of the synagogues for His name sake. *"The time cometh, that whoever killeth you will think he doeth God service."* That time came very quickly. In Acts 12:2, Herod *"killed James the brother of John with the sword."* The Apostle James was honored to be in Jesus' inner circle with his brother John and Simon Peter. On three occasions, James, John, and Peter witnessed events with Jesus that no one else got to see:

1. Jairus' daughter raised from the dead: *"And he suffered no man to follow him, save **Peter, and James, and John** the brother of James. And he cometh to the house of the ruler of the synagogue, and seeth the tumult, and them that wept and wailed greatly ... And he took the damsel by the hand, and said unto her, Talitha cumi; which is, being interpreted, Damsel, I say unto thee, arise. And straightway the damsel arose, and walked; for she was of the age of twelve years. And they were astonished with a great astonishment"* (Mark 5:37-38, 41-42).

2. The Mountain of Transfiguration: *"And after six days Jesus taketh **Peter, James, and John** his brother, and bringeth them up into an high mountain apart, And was transfigured before them: and his face did shine as the sun, and his raiment was white as the light. And, behold, there appeared unto them Moses and Elias talking with him"* (Matthew 17:1-3).

3. The agony of Jesus in the Garden of Gethsemane: *"Then cometh Jesus with them unto a place called Gethsemane, and saith unto the disciples, Sit ye here, while I go and pray yonder. And he took with him **Peter and the two sons of Zebedee**, and began to be sorrowful and very heavy"* (Matthew 26:36-37). James and John were not perfect. When they saw a Samaritan village reject Jesus, they wanted to call down fire from heaven and destroy them. Jesus rebuked them, *"Ye know not what manner of spirit ye are of"* (Luke 9:55). He also gave them a negative nickname "Boanerges" meaning "sons of thunder" (Mark 3:17). But James' love and zeal for Jesus resulted in him being the first of the apostles to be martyred. He was killed by the sword on orders given by King Herod

Agrippa I of Judea. James must have had some outstanding qualities because he was one of Jesus' favorites.

Jesus prophesied, *"They shall put you out of the synagogues: yea, the time cometh, that whosoever killeth you will think that he doeth God service"* (John 16:2). This prophecy came to pass in Acts 8:1-3, *"And Saul was consenting unto his death. And at that time there was a great persecution against the church which was at Jerusalem; and they were all scattered abroad throughout the regions of Judaea and Samaria, except the apostles. And devout men carried Stephen to his burial, and made great lamentation over him. As for Saul, he made havock of the church, entering into every house, and haling men and women committed them to prison."*

Further evidence of the need Jesus addressed in warning them is found in Acts 22:3-5: *"I am verily a man which am a Jew, born in Tarsus, a city in Cilicia, yet brought up in this city at the feet of Gamaliel, and taught according to the perfect manner of the law of the fathers, and was zealous toward God, as ye all are this day. And I persecuted this way unto the death, binding and delivering into prisons both men and women. As also the high priest doth bear me witness, and all the estate of the elders: from whom also I received letters unto the brethren, and went to Damascus, to bring them which were there bound unto Jerusalem, for to be punished."* Before Saul (Paul) of Tarsus' conversion, he persecuted the church thinking he was doing God's service. Since then, many true believers of Jesus have been persecuted and killed at the hands of those thinking they are doing God's service. Jesus said, when the time shall come, you will remember (John 16:4). He did not tell His disciples these things at the beginning, but now He is forewarning them.

THE ADVANTAGE OF THE COMFORTER'S COMING

During the earlier part of Jesus' ministry, He spoke very little about the persecution which awaited them. While the disciples traveled with Him, the hatred was directed mostly toward Jesus. But the world's hatred of Christ would soon be directed toward all His followers. In John 16:5-7, Jesus promised to send them the Comforter: *"But now I go my way to him that sent me; and none of you asketh me, Whither goest thou? But because I have said these things unto you, sorrow hath filled your heart. Nevertheless I tell you the truth;* **It is expedient for you that I go away: for if I go not away, the Comforter will not come unto you**; *but if I depart, I will send him unto you."* Sorrow filled their hearts because they could only see Jesus leaving, but Jesus said it is, *"expedient for you that I go away."* Jesus' departure was essential or necessary. It was to their advantage that He go away. This was difficult for some of the disciples to comprehend. When someone we love is near death, we might think it is better for them to go. But Jesus was saying here that it wasn't for His advantage, but for their advantage that He would go away.

Think of how difficult it must have been for them that day. What were the questions in their heart? When Jesus' ministry on earth of teaching and miracles is over, how is that to our advantage? When Jesus is arrested, how is that to our advantage? When Jesus is beaten, how is that to our advantage? When Jesus is mocked, how is that to our advantage? When Jesus is sentenced to death, how is that to our advantage? When they nailed Jesus to the cross, how is that to our advantage? When Jesus dies in shame among criminals, how is that to our advantage? When His dead body laid in a tomb, how is that to our advantage?

When Jesus said, *"It is expedient for you that I go away,"* He was saying that the dispensation of the Comforter (Holy Spirit) will be a more blessed manifestation of My presence than even that of My physical body. Jesus promising to send the Holy Spirit when He departed is what made all this to their advantage. As long as Jesus was confined in a physical body, He was limited to being at one place at any given time. It is better now because Christ can be with every believer all at the same time through His omnipresent Holy Spirit! This was not something He could do in the flesh, only by the Spirit.

All the answers as to why it was for our advantage that Jesus came and suffered are found in Isaiah 53:1-12, *"Who hath believed our report? and to whom is the arm of the Lord revealed? For he shall grow up before him as a tender plant, and as a root out of a dry ground: he hath no form nor comeliness; and when we shall see him, there is no beauty that we should desire him. He is despised and rejected of men; a man of sorrows, and acquainted with grief: and we hid as it were our faces from him; he was dewasspised, and we esteemed him not. Surely he hath borne our griefs, and carried our sorrows: yet we did esteem him stricken, smitten of God, and afflicted. But he was wounded for our transgressions, he was bruised for our iniquities: the chastisement of our peace upon him; and with his stripes we are healed. All we like sheep have gone astray; we have turned every one to his own way; and the Lord hath laid on him the iniquity of us all. He was oppressed, and he was afflicted, yet he opened not his mouth: he is brought as a lamb to the slaughter, and as a sheep before her shearers is dumb, so he openeth not his mouth. He was taken from prison and from judgment: and who shall declare his generation? for he was cut off out of the land of the living: for the transgression of my people was he stricken. And he made his grave with the wicked, and with the rich in his death; because he had done no violence, neither was any deceit in his mouth. Yet it pleased the Lord to bruise him; he hath put him to grief: when thou shalt make his soul an offering for sin, he shall see his seed, he shall prolong his days, and the pleasure of the Lord shall prosper in his hand. He shall see of the travail of his soul, and shall be satisfied: by his knowledge shall my righteous servant justify many; for he shall bear their iniquities. Therefore will I divide him a portion with the great, and he shall divide the spoil with the strong; because he hath poured out his soul unto death: and he was numbered with the transgressors; and he bare the sin of many, and made intercession for the transgressors."* Truly His leaving was advantageous for all of us!

Jesus said of the Holy Spirit, "He will reprove" or convict the world. The ancient Greek word translated "reprove" has a broader meaning than our modern word. It also carries the ideas "to expose, to refute, or to convince." We must rely on the conviction of the Holy Spirit for us to become right with God. Jesus described the work of the Holy Spirit in John 16:8-11, *"And when he is come,* **he will reprove the world of sin***, and of righteousness, and of judgment: Of sin, because they believe not on me; Of righteousness, because I go to my Father, and ye see me no more; Of judgment, because the prince of this world is judged."* The Spirit is the advocate or helper for the believer. In fact, the same Greek word translated "Comforter" four times in John's Gospel (*parakletos*) is also translated "Advocate" in 1 John 2:1 concerning Jesus. So, He is also our defense attorney—one who stands by our side to defend us. However, for the unbeliever, He is the counsel for prosecution. It's better to have the Holy Spirit defend us rather than to prosecute or convict us. Notice the phrase, *"Of sin, because they believe not on me."* The essence of sin is unbelief, which causes men to reject Jesus' words and His messengers. Consider the next phrase, *"Of righteousness, because I go to the Father."* Men had defined righteousness by the precepts of men, but now righteousness is revealed by the Holy Spirit in Jesus. The last phrase says, *"Of judgment, because the prince of this world is judged."*

The Holy Spirit is further shown to be our advocate in John 16:13-16, *"Howbeit when he, the Spirit of truth, is come, he will guide you into all truth: for he shall not speak of himself; but whatsoever he shall hear, that shall he speak: and he will shew you things to come. He shall glorify me: for he shall receive of mine, and shall shew it unto you. All things that the Father hath are mine: therefore said I, that he shall take of mine, and shall shew it unto you. A little while, and ye shall not see me: and again, a little while, and ye shall see me, because I go to the Father."* The Holy Spirit became their personal guide into all truth—the fullness of truth. John later wrote in 1 John 4:6, *"We are of God: he that knoweth God heareth us; he that is not of God heareth not us. Hereby know we the spirit of truth, and the spirit of error."*

We must listen to the Holy Spirit if we want to know the truth. Don't just search the Scriptures to prove your point, but search for truth. *"But God hath revealed them unto us by his Spirit: for **the Spirit searcheth all things, yea, the deep things of God**"* (1 Corinthians 2:10). Let the Holy Spirit lead you as you search the Scriptures. After all, the men who wrote the Scriptures did so as the Holy Spirit moved on them to write it (2 Peter 1:21). If the Holy Spirit teaches us and guides us into ALL TRUTH, then He will hold nothing back. That is sometimes hard for us to handle. He will also show us things yet to come in the future. All teaching, all preaching, all the supernatural gifts, all the writings of the apostles should have the same goal for us under the guidance and influence of the Holy Spirit. All things done by the Holy Spirit will edify the church, glorify Christ, and give instruction in righteousness.

At that time, the disciples were not able to hear all the truth. They weren't ready for it. The Holy Spirit had to gradually lead them into the Truth. Consider John 16:15, *"All things that the Father hath are mine: therefore said I, that he shall take of mine, and shall shew it unto you."* Jesus was saying what belongs to the Father belongs to Me, and what belongs to Me belongs to the Father. The Father and Son abiding together as one is shown in Colossians 1:19, *"For it pleased the Father that in him* [Jesus] *should all fulness dwell."* This could not be said if they were the same person. If you walk in union with the Holy Spirit following Christ, then all things are yours! *"Therefore let no man glory in men.* **For all things are yours**; *Whether Paul, or Apollos, or Cephas, or the world, or life, or death, or things present, or things to come;* **all are yours**; *And ye are Christ's; and Christ is God's"* (1 Corinthians 3:21-23).

Consider this verse in John 16:16, *"A little while, and ye shall not see me: and again, a little while, and ye shall see me, because I go to the Father."* The first part is speaking of the time when Jesus was in the tomb after His death— **"a little while, and ye shall not see me**.*"* The second part is referring to the time after His resurrection. This transition is seen in John 20:17, *"Jesus saith unto her, Touch me* *not;* ***for I am not yet ascended to my Father****: but go to my brethren, and say unto them, I ascend unto my Father, and your Father; and to my God, and your God."* Further description of this transition from weeping to rejoicing is seen in John 16:20, *"Verily, verily, I say unto you, That ye shall weep and lament, but the world shall rejoice: and ye shall be sorrowful, but* **your sorrow shall be turned into joy.***"* The phrase "verily, verily," is a strong way of speaking, often used by Jesus to get people to pay attention. It means "truly" or "most assuredly." Their weeping and lamenting was fulfilled in Mark 16:10, *"And she went and told them that had been with him,* **as they mourned and wept.***"* The period between the crucifixion and the resurrection was a heartbreaking experience and a dark disappointment for the disciples. These men had visions and dreams which were destroyed, seemly overnight. They suffered the loss of what they thought was their glorious future. They had dropped their jobs and livelihoods to follow Jesus. The disciples most likely thought this sorrow would never end, when in reality, it was just a short time. It was only three days, but it felt like forever. We have a hard time watching a reenactment of the Passion of Christ in our own living room. I weep every time. I cannot imagine how much sorrow they felt experiencing it for real.

SORROW TURNED INTO JOY

Next, from John 16:20, Jesus said, *"the world shall rejoice"* referring to when He was dead and gone. The chief priests and elders mocked and insulted Him. They rejoiced seeing Him hanging in agony on the cross. They thought they would not have to deal with Jesus Christ and His followers again. They were so wrong! Christ repeated again how they would be sorrowful. But then, Jesus promised,

"Your sorrow shall be turned into Joy." Can you imagine the joy unspeakable they must have felt when they first saw Jesus after the resurrection? Jesus used this analogy in John 16:21-22, *"A woman when she is in travail hath sorrow, because her hour is come: but as soon as she is delivered of the child, she remembereth no more the anguish, for joy that a man is born into the world. And ye now therefore have sorrow: but I will see you again, and your heart shall rejoice, and your joy no man taketh from you."* This is the best illustration of the pain they were going to experience. Every woman who has birthed a child will agree. According to Luke 23:27, *"There followed him a great company of people, and of women, which also bewailed and lamented him."* There were many more people than the disciples who were weeping.

Genesis 3:16 describes the pain of child birth, *"Unto the woman he said, I will greatly multiply thy sorrow and thy conception;* **in sorrow thou shalt bring forth children**; *and thy desire shall be to thy husband, and he shall rule over thee."* But as soon as a child is born, the sorrow is forgotten as a mother delivers her baby. She forgets all the pain as she gazes into the eyes of a new life. Jesus compared the situation the disciples would experience to the pain of a woman in labor or travail. Remember, Genesis 3:16 was spoken to Eve because of sin. Jesus had to suffer all this pain because of our sins. My wife said it is hard to explain. She personally experienced all the pain of childbirth. Birthing mothers go from extreme pain and agony to the most overwhelming joy and happiness. This sounds like salvation to me.

Consider the power you will receive in Jesus' name. *"And in that day ye shall ask me nothing. Verily, verily, I say unto you, Whatsoever ye shall ask the Father in my name, he will give it you"* (John 16:23). Your heart shall rejoice and your joy no man can take it from you. No persecution or trial was able to shake their faith not even death. That's why Paul wrote in Romans 8:38-39, *"For I am persuaded, that neither death, nor life, nor angels, nor principalities, nor powers, nor things present, nor things to come, Nor height, nor depth, nor any other creature, shall be able to separate us from the love of God, which is in Christ Jesus our Lord."* When Paul wrote this, he himself was facing death. He had spent months in a prison cell. Nothing could separate him from the love and joy he had in Christ Jesus his Lord. Note: the Apostle Paul was persuaded—"fully persuaded" or "fully convinced." Paul and all the apostles knew that not even physical death could separate them from the love of Christ. Death may separate us from this earth and from people we love for a while, but it is impossible for death to separate you and I from the love of Jesus. His love doesn't end with the cessation of our life. Actually, it is then we will begin to understand how endlessly He loves us.

Paul and the apostles faced all these things and here was their reward, *"And in that day ye shall ask me nothing. Verily, verily, I say unto you, Whatsoever ye shall ask the Father in my name, he will give it you. Hitherto have ye asked nothing in my name: ask, and ye shall receive, that your joy may be full. These things have I spoken unto you in proverbs: but the time cometh, when I shall no more speak unto you in proverbs, but I shall shew you plainly of the Father. At that day ye shall ask in my name: and I say not unto you, that I will pray the Father for you"* (John 16:23-26). In verse 23, He uses the phrase "verily, verily" again, emphasizing the importance of what He is about to say. In these verses, He was telling them that they can come boldly before the Father with confidence. 1 John 5:13-14 declares, *"These things have I written unto you that believe on the name of the Son of God; that ye may know that ye have eternal life, and that ye may believe on the name of the Son of God.* **And this is the confidence that we have in him**, *that, if we ask any thing according to his will, he heareth us."* When Jesus said, "In that day," He was speaking of the day after the resurrection when He became our permanent High Priest.

Hebrews 4:14-16 describes His priestly ministry, *"Seeing then that we have* **a great high priest**, *that is passed into the heavens, Jesus the Son of God, let us hold fast our profession. For we have not an high priest which cannot be touched with the feeling of Infirmities yet without sin. Let us therefore come boldly unto the throne of grace, that we may obtain mercy, and find grace to help in time of need."* He said, *"Ask the Father in my name."* To ask in the name of Jesus Christ is to ask as though Jesus Himself was asking. If we ask in His name, we should only ask what Jesus would ask. This will be addressed further in the next chapter. It's very important to pray according to the will of God. *"Ye ask, and receive not,* **because ye ask amiss**, *that ye may consume it upon your lusts"* (James 4:3). Scripture tells us not to ask selfishly for our own pleasure. If we ask selfishly, we are not asking according to His will and therefore will not receive. To truly pray is to be submissive and aware of God's will. The closer you get to your heavenly Father, the more you will take on His attitudes, His ways, and His thoughts. You will start to act and think more like Him. John 16:26 says, *"At that day ye shall ask in my name: and*

> *To truly pray is to be submissive and aware of God's will.*

I say not unto you, that I will pray the Father for you." Remember that day is when He became our permanent High Priest through His perfect sacrifice which was established by His resurrection. In the last chapter of the book, we will talk more about that.

We will see as we study, it was still hard for them to understand. Notice John 16:29-32, *"His disciples said unto him, Lo, now speakest thou plainly, and speakest no proverb. Now are we sure that thou knowest all things, and needest not that any man should ask thee: by this we believe that thou camest forth from God. Jesus answered them, Do ye now believe? Behold, the hour cometh, yea, is now come, that ye shall be scattered, every man to his own, and shall leave me alone: and yet I am not alone, because the Father is with me."* In verse 29, we see it was still hard for them to understand. When they heard, they were hearing as though it was a proverb which is like speaking in riddles. Jesus had been speaking plainly. They were confused because they never had ears to hear Him speak in such a manner before. In verse 30, they were all confessing Jesus as the Messiah. "Now we are sure you knowest all things and needest not that any man should ask thee." In essence, they were saying, although no question is asked of you, yet you answer the thoughts of every one of us. Note in verse 29, it says, *"His disciples."* Every one of them were saying this together. Further support of these ideas can be found in these verses: *"It shall come to pass, that before they call, I will answer; and while they are yet speaking, I will hear"* (Isaiah 65:24). *"Be not ye therefore like unto them: for your Father knoweth what things ye have need of, before ye ask him"* (Matthew 6:8).

Read these words of Jesus in John 16:31-33, *"Jesus answered them, Do ye now believe? Behold, the hour cometh, yea, is now come, that ye shall be scattered, every man to his own, and shall leave me alone: and yet I am not alone, because the Father is with me. These things I have spoken unto you, that in me ye might have peace. In the world ye shall have tribulation: but be of good cheer; I have overcome the world."* I don't believe as others that Jesus was rebuking them for unbelief when he said "Do ye now believe." I believe it was a question of believing the tribulation they would face. Remember, Jesus is always thinking of your future. He also knew they would be scattered. *"Then saith Jesus unto them, All ye shall be offended because of me this night: for it is written, I will smite the shepherd, and the sheep of the flock shall be scattered abroad"* (Matthew 26:31). Zechariah prophesied, *"Awake, O sword, against my shepherd, and against the man that is my fellow, saith the Lord of hosts: smite the shepherd, and the sheep shall be scattered: and I will turn mine hand upon the little ones"* (Zechariah 13:7). By being smitten, Jesus is taking the place of the Shepherd of God's people.

After the resurrection, He trained His apostles to be shepherds over God's people to fulfill the promise found in Jeremiah 3:15-17, *"And I will give you pastors according to mine heart, which shall feed you with knowledge and understanding. And it shall come to pass, when ye be multiplied and increased in the land, in those days, saith the Lord, they shall say no more, The ark of the covenant of the Lord: neither shall it come to mind: neither shall they remember it; neither shall they visit it; neither shall that be done any more. At that time they shall call Jerusalem the throne of the Lord; and all the nations shall be gathered unto it, to the name of the Lord, to Jerusalem: neither shall they walk any more after the imagination of their evil heart."* Jesus brought all of this to pass in Jerusalem after He ascended to the throne. The Ark of the Covenant represented the presence of the Lord on earth. Jeremiah was saying you won't miss the Ark anymore or visit it anymore. It won't even come to your mind. Why? Because the One the Ark of the Covenant represented (Jesus) would always be with them. Ezekiel 48:35 tells of the New Jerusalem, *"It was round about eighteen thousand measures: and the name of the city from that day shall be,* **The Lord is there**.*"* This is the passage from which we derive the divine name Jehovah-Shammah or Yahweh-Shammah. The phrase "the Lord is there" comes from this Hebrew name for God. This is speaking prophetically of the New Jerusalem—Jesus is and forever will be there! This will be further developed in later chapters of this book.

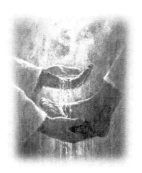

CHAPTER 5

JESUS TALKS TO HIS DADDY
(John 17)

John 17 contains the longest prayer of our Lord in the New Testament. It is only found in the Gospel of John. I believe in this prayer that Jesus prayed to the Father. He was probably standing with His hands lifted to the Father and His eyes were looking toward heaven. Jesus prayed this prayer with the intention of the disciples hearing Him. This is known as Jesus' great intercessory prayer for the church. This prayer, I believe, was a conversational prayer with two talking back and forth to one another. It was a dialogue between the Father and the Son (Jesus). I believe this prayer was much longer than what is recorded. Do you wonder what the disciples were thinking when they heard Jesus praying to the Father, then pausing quietly to listen to the Father? They couldn't hear the Father. They only heard what Jesus was saying. *"These words spake Jesus, and lifted up his eyes to heaven, and said, Father, the hour is come; glorify thy Son, that thy Son also may glorify thee"* (John 17:1).

This is one of the many times Jesus was found in prayer. Jesus' ministry began in prayer. *"Now when all the people were baptized, it came to pass, that Jesus also being baptized, **and praying**, the heaven was opened"* (Luke 3:21).

Most preachers talk only of His baptism, but they forget to stress that Jesus was praying when heaven opened up. Why did the voice that came from heaven say, "Thou art my beloved son, in whom I am well pleased?" Whose voice was that? It was the voice of the Father. Jesus was talking to the Father by praying, and the Father responded by speaking back to Jesus. What caused the Father to say, *"This is my beloved Son, in whom I am well pleased?"*

Here is the story recorded in Matthew 3:13-17, *"Then cometh Jesus from Galilee to Jordan unto John, to be baptized of him. But John forbad him, saying, I have need to be baptized of thee, and comest thou to me? And Jesus answering said unto him, suffer it to be so now: for thus it becometh us to fulfil all righteousness. Then he suffered him. And Jesus, when he was baptized, went up straightway out of the water: and, lo, the heavens were opened unto him, and he saw the Spirit of God descending like a dove, and lighting upon him: And lo a voice from heaven, saying, This is my beloved Son, in whom I am well pleased."* Notice the phrase "to fulfill all righteousness." Righteousness means obedience to or right standing with God. The word "all" emphasizes that Jesus' baptism was to fulfill the law and to obtain "righteousness" for "all" humanity. John's baptism was for sinners, not for the righteousness. *"John did baptize in the wilderness, and preach* **the baptism of repentance for the remission of sins"** (Mark 1:4). People *"were baptized of him in Jordan,* **confessing their sins"** (Matthew 3:6). Jesus was sinless, so He didn't need to be baptized for Himself. He did it to fulfill the law and to set the example for all those who would follow Him.

Take a close look at the following verses: *"The next day John seeth Jesus coming unto him, and saith, Behold the Lamb of God, which taketh away the sin of the world. This is he of whom I said, After me cometh a man which is preferred before me: for he was before me. And I knew him not: but that he should be made manifest to Israel, therefore am I come baptizing with water. And John bare record, saying, I saw the Spirit descending from heaven like a dove, and it abode upon him. And I knew him not: but he that sent me to baptize with water, the same said unto me, Upon whom thou shalt see the Spirit descending, and remaining on him, the same is he which baptizeth with the Holy Ghost. And I saw, and bare record that this is the Son of God"* (John 1:29-34). John declared Jesus as the spotless (without blemish) Lamb of God. John the Baptist was a priest with a Levitical heritage. His father, Zacharias, was of the course of Abiah (one of Samuel's sons—1 Samuel 8:2) and his mother, Elizabeth, was of the daughters of Aaron (Luke 1:5). So, both priestly lines of the Old Covenant (the Levitical priesthood and the priesthood of Samuel) converged in John the Baptist. Here was a priest declaring (before baptism) that Jesus was clean and accepted by God. When John said earlier, *"I am not worthy to untie His sandals,"* he was confessing his own sinful condition. Anything to do with feet was usually reserved for the lowest slave. Sometimes we study God's action, but God's ways are usually contrary to what we think. To be called the Lamb of God meant that, from that day on, Jesus was like a lamb being led to the slaughter (reserved for sacrifice).

Jesus was chosen from the foundation of the world to be slain, but the priest had to declare, "The Lamb of God." John had inspected Jesus for 30 years, but found no spot or blemish, or any sin in Jesus. Israel was not truly a nation until the night they were delivered from Egypt's bondage.

That night, they put the blood of a lamb on the door posts and the lintels of each house. We were not a holy nation until the Lamb's blood was shed for us. The night they came out, they came out as a free nation. So, Jesus did not get baptism for His sins, but ours. God gave John the Baptist witness that Jesus was indeed the Messiah.

Jesus was chosen from the foundation of the world to be slain.

Jesus "fulfilled all righteousness" for our sins, not His own. This symbolized His future death. This is why we should be baptized—to identify with the death, burial, and resurrection of Christ (Romans 6:3-5). Jesus was baptized in the Jordan River. Jordan means "descending or death." In Bible typology, the Jordan River is a symbol of death. This series of events—Jesus being baptized, praying, and the Father speaking to Him were proclaiming that He and the Father were one!

THE "I AM" STATEMENTS OF JESUS

After the Father declared "This is my beloved Son in whom I Am" over Jesus, then Jesus declared Himself as the "I Am" nine times in the Gospel of John:

1. *"And Jesus said unto them,* **I am the bread of life**: *he that cometh to me shall never hunger; and he that believeth on me shall never thirst"*—John 6:35.

2. *"Then spake Jesus again unto them, saying,* **I am the light of the world**: *he that followeth me shall not walk in darkness, but shall have the light of life"*—John 8:12.

3. *"Jesus said unto them, Verily, verily, I say unto you, **Before Abraham was, I am**"*—John 8:58.

4. *"**I am the door**: by me if any man enter in, he shall be saved, and shall go in and out, and find pasture"*—John 10:9.

5. *"**I am the good shepherd**: the good shepherd giveth his life for the sheep"*—John 10:11.

6. *"Jesus said unto her, **I am the resurrection, and the life**: he that believeth in me, though he were dead, yet shall he live: And whosoever liveth and believeth in me shall never die. Believest thou this?"*—John 11:25-26.

7. *"Jesus saith unto him, **I am the way, the truth, and the life**: no man cometh unto the Father, but by me"*—John 14:6.

8. *"**I am the vine, ye are the branches**: He that abideth in me, and I in him, the same bringeth forth much fruit: for without me ye can do nothing"*—John 15:5.

9. *"Jesus therefore, knowing all things that should come upon him, went forth, and said unto them, Whom seek ye? They answered him, Jesus of Nazareth. Jesus saith unto them, **I am he**. And ... as soon then as he had said unto them, **I am he**, they went backward, and fell to the ground"*—John 18:4-6.

Let's go back to John 17. Jesus was praying a High Priestly Prayer of Intercession for His disciples. There are three parts to that prayer which we will look at:

1. Jesus Prayed for Himself. *"These words spake*

Jesus, and lifted up his eyes to heaven, and said, Father, the hour is come; **glorify thy Son, that thy Son also may glorify thee**: *As thou hast given him power over all flesh, that he should give eternal life to as many as thou hast given him. And this is life eternal, that they might know thee the only true God, and Jesus Christ, whom thou hast sent. I have glorified thee on the earth: I have finished the work which thou gavest me to do. And now, O Father, glorify thou me with thine own self with the glory which I had with thee before the world was"* (John 17:1-5).

Jesus prayed for Himself first, but He was in no way being selfish. Someone said it is selfish to pray for yourself, but Jesus unselfishly prayed for Himself. If Jesus prayed for Himself, then we can and should too. But we must do it unselfishly. The prayer must not be for personal gain but for the advancement of God's kingdom. "I pray for the Father to glorify thy Son." Why? "That the Son may glorify the Father." That's unselfish. In verses 2-3, Jesus prayed unselfishly to be glorified so that He could give eternal life to many. Someone asked, what is eternal life? Jesus answered, "that they know the Father and the Son." Pastor Harold Mash once said, "Eternal Life" is "time spent with God." I agree. Jesus acknowledged that He had power over all flesh, including over all humanity. Jesus had full authority over Judas Iscariot, over the High Priest, over the Sanhedrin Court, over Pontius Pilate, and over the mob that cried, "crucify Him." He had authority over the cross, over death, hell, and the grave before He ever faced them, all that we might be saved. Every time someone gets saved, Jesus and the Father receive more Glory.

"Ye men of Israel, hear these words; Jesus of Nazareth, a man approved of God among you by miracles and wonders and signs, which God did by him in the midst of you,

as ye yourselves also know: Him, being delivered by the determinate counsel and foreknowledge of God, ye have taken, and by wicked hands have crucified and slain" (Acts 2:22-23). We understand that all the things that happened to Jesus were part of the predetermined plan and with the foreknowledge of God the Father. Jesus knew it all would happen from the foundation of the world. *"And all that dwell upon the earth shall worship him, whose names are not written in the book of life of* **the Lamb slain from the foundation of the world**" (Revelations 13:8). Read John 17:5 again, *"And now, O Father, glorify thou me with thine own self with the glory which I had with thee before the world was."* Jesus was also glorified in His resurrection as "the firstfruits of them that slept" (1 Corinthians 15:20-22) on the Day of Firstfruits, and His exaltation to heaven until the time of the restitution of all things. *"Whom the heaven must receive until* **the times of restitution of all things**, *which God hath spoken by the mouth of all his holy prophets since the world began"* (Acts 3:21). Since the Day of Pentecost, He has been glorified in His people.

2. Jesus Prayed for His Disciples. *"I have manifested thy name unto the men which thou gavest me out of the world: thine they were, and thou gavest them me; and they have kept thy word. Now they have known that all things whatsoever thou hast given me are of thee. For I have given unto them the words which thou gavest me; and they have received them, and have known surely that I came out from thee, and they have believed that thou didst send me.* **I pray for them: I pray not for the world, but for them which thou hast given me; for they are thine**. *And all mine are thine, and thine are mine; and I am glorified in them. And now I am no more in the world,* but these are in the world, and I come to thee. Holy Father, keep through thine own name those whom thou hast given me, that they may be one, as we are. While I was with them in the world, I kept them in thy name: those that thou gavest me I have kept, and none of them is lost, but the son of perdition; that the scripture might be fulfilled. And now come I to thee; and these things I speak in the world, that they might have my joy fulfilled in themselves. I have given them thy word; and the world hath hated them, because they are not of the world, even as I am not of the world. I pray not that thou shouldest take them out of the world, but that thou shouldest keep them from the evil. They are not of the world, even as I am not of the world. Sanctify them through thy truth: thy word is truth. As thou hast sent me into the world, even so have I also sent them into the world. And for their sakes I sanctify myself, that they also might be sanctified through the truth"* (John 17:6-19).

In these verses, Jesus mentions what was given to Him by the Father. Jesus also speaks of His pre-existence before He was sent into the world. In these verses, many terms refer to the act of giving. Both the Father and the Son are "givers." *"For God so loved the world, **that he gave his only begotten Son**, that whosoever believeth in him should not perish, but have everlasting life"* (John 3:16). Like Father, like Son. As the Father is a giver, so is the Son. In verses 6, 11, and 12, Jesus manifested His name. He keeps His disciples through the Father's name. What is the Father's name? While there are many divine names and titles that reveal different aspects of God's character and nature, one of the greatest is found in Exodus 3:14, *"And God said unto Moses, **I AM THAT I AM**: and he said, Thus shalt thou say unto the children of Israel, I AM hath* *sent me unto you."* "I Am" is the Father's names He spoke over Jesus at His baptism. The Father gave that name to Jesus. In the Gospel of John, as shown in the list above, you find a direct connection between Jehovah I AM of the Old Testament and Jesus I AM in the New Testament. When Christ appeared to Saul in a blinding light, he asked Him, *"Who art thou, Lord? And the Lord said,* **I am Jesus** *whom thou persecutest: it is hard for thee to kick against the pricks"* (Acts 9:5).

What happened at the Jordan River that day is what we would call "the adoption of a son." There has been much error taught concerning "adoption and sonship" in the body of Christ mostly because we have looked at biblical adoption through the eyes of our western culture. The biblical (Hebrew) view of the "adoption of a son" has absolutely nothing to do with the placement of an orphan into a foster home. Rather, it has to do with a young man coming into a place of maturity, receiving the full authority, and resources of his father bestowed upon him. Through Jesus, the Father adopted us as sons with full rights and authority. Paul explained, *"For as many as are led by the Spirit of God, they are the sons of God. For ye have not received the spirit of bondage again to fear; but* **ye have received the Spirit of adoption, whereby we cry,** **Abba, Father.** *The Spirit itself beareth witness with our spirit, that we are the children of God: And if children, then heirs; heirs of God, and joint-heirs with Christ; if so be that we suffer with him, that we may be also glorified together. For I reckon that the sufferings of this present time are not worthy to be compared with the glory which shall be revealed in us. For the earnest expectation of the creature waiteth for the manifestation of the sons of God. For the creature was made subject to vanity, not willingly,* *but by reason of him who hath subjected the same in hope, Because the creature itself also shall be delivered from the bondage of corruption into the glorious liberty of the children of God. For we know that the whole creation groaneth and travaileth in pain together until now. And not only they, but ourselves also, which have the firstfruits of the Spirit, even we ourselves groan within ourselves, waiting for the adoption, to wit, the redemption of our body"* (Romans 8:14-23).

There are three stages of growth in the life of a Jewish young boy. We can see these stages by looking into the life of our Savior, Jesus Christ. In the first stage, Jesus was born and circumcised on the eighth day. This is the infant stage. His circumcision marked Him as a "son of the covenant" and was celebrated throughout the family and community. *"And when eight days were accomplished for the circumcising of the child, his name was called Jesus, which was so named of the angel before he was conceived in the womb"* (Luke 2:21). This was His calling!

The second stage was Jesus' "Bar Mitzvah," which took place as he was about to enter puberty. *"And when he was twelve years old, they went up to Jerusalem after the custom of the feast"* (Luke 2:42). This was a very special event as it still is today among the Jewish people! You should be in Israel to see a "Bar Mitzvah!" The youth is lifted upon his father's shoulder and carried throughout the street. The men will dance with him and the Lord also dances with us! The young boy will dance with the Torah (the first five books of the Bible) which he can now quote from memory. The word "Bar Mitzvah" means the "Son of Commandment" or "Son of Accountability." By this time, a youth should do his schoolwork and room responsibilities without being told to do it! The youth was held accountable to keep the "Commandments of God" as modeled by keeping the commandments of his father. He would become an apprentice under his father in the family business. What did Jesus say after His Bar Mitzvah when Joseph and Mary found Him in the Temple? *"Wist ye not that I must be about **my Father's business**"* (Luke 2:49). This was His election!

In the third stage, Jesus was about to reach thirty years old. *"Now when all the people were baptized, it came to pass, that Jesus also being baptized, and praying, the heaven was opened, And the Holy Ghost descended in a bodily shape like a dove upon him, and a voice came from heaven, which said, Thou art my beloved Son; in thee I am well pleased.* **And Jesus himself began to be about thirty years of age**, *being (as was supposed) the son of Joseph"* (Luke 3:21-23). At this time, the Jewish father of the youth would place his hand upon the head of his son and openly proclaim, "This is my Beloved Son in whom I am well pleased!" At this time, the father would bestow upon his son all of his riches and the power and authority to act on behalf of his father in all his affairs. By now you could see his father in him! This was Him being Chosen!

Can you see through these three stages our own spiritual growth requires us to become sons? Can you now understand why Jesus said to His mother at twelve years of age, "Know ye not that I must be about My Father's business?" Can you see that He was proclaiming His apprenticeship (discipleship, training for ministry) under His heavenly Father? Can you see when He was about thirty years of age, He received the "spirit of sonship" or "the adoption" as the "Son of God?" Jesus never declared "I Am" before this day. His adoption at the Jordan River was done to "fulfill all righteousness" and then He began His public ministry. The Father proclaimed before all, "This is my beloved Son in whom I am well pleased." *"Wherefore thou art no more a servant, but a son; and if a son, then an heir of God through Christ"* (Galatians 4:7).

When you hear someone pray out loud as Jesus did in John 17, you will learn much about them. In the previous verses, Jesus' prayer reveals His preexistence with the Father (verses 4, 5, 18, 24). Jesus the Son and the Father (I Am) are one (verses 10, 11, 21, 22). Jesus carrying out His purpose while He was on earth is demonstrated (verses 2, 4, 6, 8, 18).

Jesus came with a clear Word from the Father (verse 8). Jesus knew He was about to suffer greatly, yet His prayers were for others even when He prayed for Himself. You cannot pray a prayer of intercession selfishly. He knew what He was facing, yet He prayed for the protection of His disciples and keeping away from the evil one—*"I pray not that thou shouldest take them out of the world,* **but that thou shouldest keep them from the evil"** (John 17:15).

3. Jesus Prayed for Unity Among His Disciples. What I take away from this prayer is Jesus' greatest desire was and is for His disciples to have unity. His command is that His family would be one and love one another. What is the glory that the Father gives the Son and the Son gives us? *"And* **the glory** *which thou gavest me I have given them; that they may be one, even as we are one"* (John 17:22). I believe that every time the word "glory" or "glorify" is mentioned in John 17,

> Jesus' greatest desire was and is for His disciples to have unity.

they are referring to the Holy Spirit. The work of the Holy Spirit is to reveal the glory of God and to glorify Jesus. When Jesus is glorified, He will share that Glory with us. *"He that believeth on me, as the scripture hath said, out of his belly shall flow rivers of living water. (But this spake he of the Spirit, which they that believe on him should receive: for the Holy Ghost was not yet given; because that **Jesus was not yet glorified**)"* (John 7:38-39).

Believers would receive the Holy Spirit after Jesus was glorified. The Greek word for "belly" found here means "belly, womb or a cavity." Other versions render it "out of his innermost being or heart." The womb is the place where the seed is conceived and nourished until birth. *"And it came to pass, that, when Elisabeth heard the salutation of Mary, the babe leaped in her womb; and Elisabeth was filled with the Holy Ghost: And she spake out with a loud voice, and said, Blessed art thou among women, and blessed is the fruit of thy womb"* (Luke 1:41-42). *"When as his mother Mary was espoused to Joseph, before they came together, she was found with child of the Holy Ghost"* (Matthew 1:18). You can clearly see the Holy Spirit (Living Water) is in the womb of Elizabeth. Babies in the womb need oxygen. Developing babies are surrounded by amniotic fluid and their lungs are filled with the fluid. By 10-12 weeks, the babies begin to practice taking breaths. The lungs have no oxygen, and only refill the lungs with more amniotic fluid. The oxygen is supplied through the umbilical cord. There is no other way for the baby to breathe. Paul made this connection, *"My little children, of whom I travail in birth again until Christ be formed in you"* (Galatians 4:19).

The Holy Spirit is very involved with the spiritual birth. *"Jesus answered and said unto him, Verily, verily, I say unto* thee, Except a man be born again, he cannot see the kingdom of God. Nicodemus saith unto him, How can a man be born when he is old? can he enter the second time into his mother's womb, and be born? Jesus answered, Verily, verily, I say unto thee, **Except a man be born of water and of the Spirit**, he cannot enter into the kingdom of God. That which is born of the flesh is flesh; and **that which is born of the Spirit is spirit**. Marvel not that I said unto thee, Ye must be born again. The wind bloweth where it listeth, and thou hearest the sound thereof, but canst not tell whence it cometh, and whither it goeth: **so is every one that is born of the Spirit**" (John 3:3-8). Jesus wants to make us part of His family as Paul wrote, *"For this cause I bow my knees unto the Father of our Lord Jesus Christ,* **Of whom the whole family in heaven and earth is named***, That he would grant you, according to the riches of his glory, to be strengthened with might by his Spirit in the inner man; That Christ may dwell in your hearts by faith; that ye, being rooted and grounded in love, May be able to comprehend with all saints what is the breadth, and length, and depth, and height; And to know the love of Christ, which passeth knowledge, that ye might be filled with all the fulness of God"* (Ephesians 3:14-19).

This is how we become part of His family. The Holy Spirit is the glory—our Living Water. Our new birth is not getting a new religion but receiving a new life (becoming a new creation) in this the world. *"Therefore if any man be in Christ,* **he is a new creature***: old things are passed away; behold, all things are become new"* (2 Corinthians 5:17). Read these verses with the understanding that the Holy Spirit is the glory of God. *"But we all, with open face beholding as in a glass the glory of the Lord, are changed into the same image* **from glory to glory***,* **even as by the**

Spirit of the Lord" (2 Corinthians 3:18). From glory (the manifestation of the Holy Spirit) to another glory (greater manifestation of the Holy Spirit). *"For God, who commanded the light to shine out of darkness, hath shined in our hearts, to give the light of the knowledge of* **the glory of God in the face of Jesus Christ**" (2 Corinthians 4:6). These verses prove that Paul refers to the Holy Spirit by the name of "glory!" Glory, Presence, Spirit are all names for the Holy Spirit. *"Even the Spirit of truth; whom the world cannot receive, because it seeth him not, neither knoweth him: but ye know him; for he dwelleth with you, and shall be in you"* (John 4:17). *"For it pleased the Father that in him should all fulness dwell"* (Colossians 1:19). The Son and the Spirit work together to reveal the glory of the Father.

We will finish with the last verse which speaks for itself, *"And I have declared unto them thy name, and will declare it: that the love wherewith thou hast loved me may be in them, and I in them"* (John 17:26). Jesus' prayer in John 17 reveals His servant heart and unselfish desire to equip His disciples for an empowered and success filled ministry!

CHAPTER 6

JESUS DRINKS THE CUP OF WRATH
(John 18)

In John 17, we saw Jesus as fully God communing with His Father. In John 18, we will see Jesus as fully man crying out to His Father. Jesus had to be fully man so that He could identify with us, suffering in our place and sympathizing with us in our weakness. John 18:1 informs us, *"When Jesus had spoken these words, he went forth with his disciples over the brook Cedron, where was a garden, into the which he entered, and his disciples."* What was the name of the garden that Jesus and His disciples entered into after leaving Jerusalem? Mark 14:32 provides the answer, *"And they came to a place which was named **Gethsemane**: and he saith to his disciples, Sit ye here, while I shall pray."* Luke 22:39 gives us another detail, *"And he came out, and went, as he was wont, to the **mount of Olives**; and his disciples also followed him."* The name of the garden was Gethsemane which was located at the base of the Mount of Olives, and it was one of Jesus' favorite places to rest.

Mark 14:33-42 describes what happened next, *"And he taketh with him Peter and James and John, and began to be sore amazed, and to be very heavy. And saith unto them, My soul is exceeding sorrowful unto death: tarry ye here, and watch. And he went forward a little, and fell on the ground, and prayed that, if it were possible, the hour might pass from him. And he said, Abba, Father, all things are possible unto thee; take away this cup from me: nevertheless not what I will, but what thou wilt. And he cometh, and findeth them sleeping, and saith unto Peter, Simon, sleepest thou? couldest not thou watch one hour? Watch ye and pray, lest ye enter into temptation. The spirit truly is ready, but the flesh is weak. And again he went away, and prayed, and spake the same words. And when he returned, he found them asleep again, (for their eyes were heavy,) neither wist they what to answer him. And he cometh the third time, and saith unto them, Sleep on now, and take your rest: it is enough, the hour is come; behold, the Son of man is betrayed into the hands of sinners. Rise up, let us go; lo, he that betrayeth me is at hand."*

Gethsemane means "an oil press." Jesus often resorted to this garden with His disciples when He ministered in or near Jerusalem. Jesus told eight of the disciples to sit at the entrance; but He took Peter, James, and John further into the garden. He told them to stay where they were as He went a little further. He told the three (His inner circle), *"My soul is exceedingly sorrowful unto death."* The word "sorrowful" literally means "ringed around with sorrow," meaning "sorrow had shut Him in." Luke 22:44 describes the intense pressure Jesus endured, *"And being in an agony he prayed more earnestly: and* **his sweat was as it were great drops of blood** *falling down to the ground."* His prayer and sorrow were so intense that Jesus He suffered what doctors call Hematohidrosis. This is a medical condition that occurs when someone is under extreme stress. When someone experiences extreme stress, the capillaries that go to the sweat glands rupture causing the blood from the capillaries to pour into the sweat glands. This is what happened to Jesus. From the Garden of Gethsemane, the blood of Jesus began being shed.

At this point, Jesus will begin to drink the cup of wrath of the Father for us. Jesus prayed three times to the Father, *"If it be possible, let this cup pass from me."* In John 17, it was the part of Jesus that was fully God praying, but now it was the part of Jesus that is fully man crying out in agony. Jesus was required to drink the entire cup, fully knowing how bitter it would be. In the same prayer or breath, He adds, *"Nevertheless, not my will, but thy will be done."* At this point, the part of Jesus that was fully man was in total submission to God's will. *"And he went a little further, and fell on his face, and prayed, saying, O my Father, if it be possible, let this cup pass from me: nevertheless not as I will, but as thou wilt"* (Matthew 26:39). A few moments later, *"He went away again the second time, and prayed, saying, O my Father, if this cup may not pass away from me, except I drink it, thy will be done"* (Matthew 26:42).

Jesus' nature as a man was perfect, yet He recoiled from the thought of the cup of wrath He had to drink. As Jesus began to drink this cup of wrath, He began to fulfill on our behalf 2 Corinthians 5:21—*"For he hath made him to be sin for us, who knew no sin; that we might be made the righteousness of God in him."* Jesus had never tasted of sin. But now, He was beginning to drink from a massive cup of filth. This cup was not just full of every sin past, present, and future, but it was sin itself. Have you ever tried to drink something that you hated? It takes what seems like forever to finish it. Because of this cup, He would be temporarily separated from His Father. That was a major reason for His agony. As much as Jesus hates sin, to drink of it shows He loves us more. Jesus did not finish the cup until He was on the cross, *"When Jesus therefore had received the vinegar, he said, It is finished: and he bowed his head, and gave up the ghost"* (John 19:30).

Jesus slowly drank the cup of wrath from Gethsemane up to His last words on the cross, "It is finished." The first time they offered Jesus vinegar wine, He would not drink it. *"They gave him vinegar to drink mingled with gall: and when he had tasted thereof, he would not drink"* (Matthew 27:34). As Jesus neared death, He cried out, "I thirst" as John 19:28 records, *"After this, Jesus knowing that all things were now accomplished, that the scripture might be fulfilled, saith, I thirst."* After finishing a cup of something bitter, you need something else to drink to get the bitter taste out of your mouth. Jesus had finished the cup of wrath and wanted that taste out of His mouth.

This was prophesied in Psalm 69:21 centuries earlier, *"They gave me also gall for my meat; and in my thirst they gave me vinegar to drink."* After Jesus cried "I thirst" from the cross, *"Now there was set a vessel full of vinegar: and they filled a spunge with vinegar, and put it upon hyssop, and put it to his mouth. When Jesus therefore had received the vinegar, he said, It is finished: and he bowed his head, and gave up the ghost"* (John 19:29-30). When Jesus received the vinegar to remove the taste, He said, "It is finished," bowed His head, and gave up the ghost. The vinegar was offered to Jesus on a sponge put on hyssop. Hyssop was a bush, or a shrub used to sprinkle blood or to transfer the effects of a sacrifice. The Children of Israel used hyssop plants like a primitive paintbrush to apply lamb's blood to their doorposts in Exodus 12:22, *"And ye shall take* **a bunch of hyssop, and dip it in the blood** *that is in the bason, and strike the lintel and the two side* posts with the blood that is in the bason; and none of you shall go out at the door of his house until the morning." In David's psalm of repentance, He asked God to *"**Purge me with hyssop**, and I shall be clean: wash me, and I shall be whiter than snow"* (Psalm 51:7).

GETHSEMANE'S OIL PRESS

Let us return to the Garden of Gethsemane. Jesus told the disciples, *"The spirit is willing, but the flesh is weak."* It was His Spirit that was willing, and His flesh that was weak. Jesus was not speaking of just the disciple's spirit and their flesh but also of His own. *"Watch and pray, that ye enter not into temptation: the spirit indeed is willing, but the flesh is weak"* (Matthew 26:41). Jesus was battling with the flesh just like we do. *"Then saith he unto them, My soul is exceeding sorrowful, even unto death: tarry ye here, and watch with me"* (Matthew 26:38). Jesus was overwhelmed with sorrow to the point of death. In the Garden of Gethsemane there was an oil press where they would crush the olives to separate the oil (anointing) from the skin (flesh) of the olive.

> *Jesus was not speaking of just the disciple's spirit and their flesh but also of His own.*

Isaiah 53:5, 10 prophesied how Jesus would be bruised or crushed like an olive for us, *"But **he was wounded for our transgressions**, **he was bruised for our iniquities**: the chastisement of our peace was upon him; and with his stripes we are healed … Yet **it pleased the Lord to bruise him**; he hath put him to grief: when thou shalt make his soul an offering for sin, he shall see his seed, he shall prolong his days, and the pleasure of the Lord shall prosper in his hand."* Jesus knew what was ahead of Him. *"And* *he began to teach them, that the Son of man must suffer many things, and be rejected of the elders, and of the chief priests, and scribes, and be killed, and after three days rise again"* (Mark 8:31). In Gethsemane, Jesus conquered the flesh and kept it in subjection to the Spirit. The battle Jesus went through was not sinful. He knew no sin. It was a human struggle. *"Wherefore in all things it behoved him to be made like unto his brethren, that he might be a merciful and faithful high priest in things pertaining to God, to make reconciliation for the sins of the people"* (Hebrews 2:17).

Remember John 18:3-6? *"Judas then, having received a band of men and officers from the chief priests and Pharisees, cometh thither with lanterns and torches and weapons. Jesus therefore, knowing all things that should come upon him, went forth, and said unto them, Whom seek ye? They answered him, Jesus of Nazareth. Jesus saith unto them, I am he. And Judas also, which betrayed him, stood with them. As soon then as he had said unto them, I am he, they went backward, and fell to the ground."* How many soldiers do you need to arrest one man? Judas brought a "band of men." In those days, a band of men consisted of a military group of 300 to 600 soldiers. Also, with Judas were officers from the chief priest. These would have been the police who guarded the Temple grounds. All these were highly trained men. The garden was filled with soldiers and police. Matthew 26:47 sets the scene, *"And while he yet spake, lo, Judas, one of the twelve, came, and with him a great multitude with swords and staves, from the chief priests and elders of the people."* Mark's account agrees, *"And immediately, while he yet spake, cometh Judas, one of the twelve, and with him a great multitude with swords and staves, from the chief priests and the scribes and the elders"* (Mark 14:43). A multitude of armed men indicates a massive army. They came with lanterns, torches, and weapons. Jesus asked, "whom do you seek?" They replied, "Jesus of Nazareth." In verses 5 and 6 of John 18, Jesus said, "I am He!" Do you remember what I said in the last chapter? I Am refers to the Father by one of His divine names. It also refers to Jesus the Son—"I Am Jesus." The soldiers with the numbers and weapons were expecting Jesus to cower in fear. Look again at John 18:6, *"As soon then as he had said unto them,* **I am he***, they went backward, and* **fell to the ground***."* Judas and all the soldiers were laying all over the garden demonstrating how every knee will bow to Jesus' lordship!

Let's jump ahead and look at John 18:10-11, *"Then Simon Peter having a sword drew it, and smote the high priest's servant, and cut off his right ear. The servant's name was Malchus. Then said Jesus unto Peter, Put up thy sword into the sheath: the cup which my Father hath given me, shall I not drink it?"* Also, let's look at Luke 22:35-38, *"And he said unto them, When I sent you without purse, and scrip, and shoes, lacked ye any thing? And they said, Nothing. Then said he unto them, But now, he that hath a purse, let him take it, and likewise his scrip: and he that hath no sword, let him sell his garment, and buy one For I say unto you, that this that is written must yet be accomplished in me, And he was reckoned among the transgressors: for the things concerning me have an end. And they said, Lord, behold, here are two swords. And he said unto them, It is enough."*

Take a closer look at this, Jesus asked, *"When I sent you without purse, bag, or sandals, did you lack anything?"* They replied, "Nothing." Look at what He told them to do next in verse 36—"buy a sword." The disciples produced two swords. Then Jesus said unto them, "It is enough." Have you who are parents ever said, "that is enough?" Jesus knew all things. He knew what was going to happen in the Garden of Gethsemane just like He knew Peter would deny Him. Jesus knew the multitude would be coming to arrest Him. *"Jesus therefore,* **knowing all things that should come upon him***, went forth, and said unto them, Whom seek ye?"* (John 18:4)

Do you really believe Jesus was telling His disciples that two swords were enough? Peter's attack is symbolic of Peter's misunderstanding of Jesus' Kingship and His kingdom. Peter must have thought because they saw the men fall backward to the ground when Jesus said "I AM He" that they could truly win with two swords. Notice Luke 22:49-50, *"When they which were about him saw what would follow, they said unto him,* **Lord, shall we smite with the sword***? And one of them smote the servant of the high priest, and cut off his right ear."* Peter asked Jesus if they should strike, but he didn't even wait for an answer. A lot of us are like Peter. In the middle of all Jesus was suffering, He stopped to show mercy to Malchus by healing his ear.

Jesus rebuked Peter for the same reason He had before in Matthew 16:22-25, *"Then Peter took him, and began to rebuke him, saying, Be it far from thee, Lord: this shall not be unto thee. But he turned, and said unto Peter,* **Get thee behind me***,* **Satan***:* **thou art an offence unto me: for thou savourest not the things that be of God, but those that be of men***. Then said Jesus unto his disciples, If any man will come after me, let him deny himself, and take up his cross, and follow me. For whosoever will save his life shall lose it: whosoever will lose his life for my sake shall find it."* Peter was thinking as we do most of the time, like all other people think. Instead, we should allow the Holy Spirit to lead us into thinking the way God thinks!

Jesus was led away to stand trial before Annas, *"And led him away to Annas first; for he was father in law to Caiaphas, which was the high priest that same year. Now Caiaphas was he, which gave and counsel to the Jews, that it was expedient that one man should die for the people"* (John 18:13-14). Christ was brought before an earthly high priest to be condemned for our blasphemies, that we might be acquitted by our everlasting High Priest— Jesus Christ our Lord. *"And Simon Peter followed Jesus, and so did another disciple: that disciple was known unto the high priest, and went in with Jesus into the palace of the high priest"* (John 18:15). The other disciple was John and he alone went in with Jesus before the High Priest *"But Peter stood at the door without. Then went out that other disciple, which was known unto the high priest, and spake unto her that kept the door, and brought in Peter"* (John 18:16). John had some connections because he knew Caiaphas, the High Priest, and was given access to his palace where Jesus' trial was held, and he helped Peter get inside the compound too.

PETER'S DENIAL

Next, John recorded Peter's denial of Christ, *"Then saith the damsel that kept the door unto Peter, Art not thou also one of this man's disciples? He saith, I am not. And the servants and officers stood there, who had made a fire of coals; for it was cold: and they warmed themselves: and Peter stood with them, and warmed himself … And Simon Peter stood and warmed himself. They said therefore unto him, Art not thou also one of his disciples? He denied it, and said, I am not. One of the servants of the high priest, being his kinsman whose ear Peter cut off, saith, Did not I see thee in the garden with him? Peter then denied again: and immediately the cock crew"* (John 18:17-18, 25-27). In Peter's denial of Jesus there is one thing I would like to point out to you. Peter at-

> When we try to blend in with the world, we will most likely end up denying our Lord.

tempted to blend in with the very ones who had arrested Jesus. When we try to blend in with the world, we will most likely end up denying our Lord.

First, in verse 17, Peter is recognized by a servant girl, but Peter denied his association with Jesus. John showed no concern for what the crowd thought of his association with Jesus. Then, in verse 18, Peter did not want to leave Jesus, but he was still blending in and being a coward among the crowd who arrested Jesus. Peter's second denial came in verse 25. Again, he denied it and said, "I am not." A few hours earlier, Peter had said he would die for Jesus, but now he is denying Him. Peter's third denial is found in verses 26-27. The third person to question Peter was a relative of Malchus, the man whose ear Peter had cut off. Peter denied His association with Jesus again, and then the cock crowed. Jesus, you recall, prophesied Peter's denial in the upper room after the Last Supper—*"Jesus answered him, Wilt thou lay down thy life for my sake? Verily, verily, I say unto thee, The cock shall not crow, till thou hast denied me thrice"* (John 13:38). *Jesus prepared Peter for this event, "And the Lord said, Simon, Simon, behold, Satan hath desired to have you, that he may sift you as wheat:* **But I have prayed for thee, that thy faith fail not**: *and when thou art converted, strengthen thy brethren"* (Luke 22:31-32).

The reason Peter survived this is because Jesus had prayed for him. The Apostle John did not mention in his account Peter's oaths, cursing, or the bitter tears as did the other Gospels. *"And Peter remembered the word of Jesus, which said unto him, Before the cock crow, thou shalt deny me thrice.* **And he went out, and wept bitterly**" (Matthew 26:75). This was a godly sorrow that led Peter to repentance. Jesus had prayed for Peter even before his denial. Jesus forgave Peter and never mentioned it directly to him but He did give Peter a test later in John 21:15-19 after His resurrection just like Joseph did his brothers in Egypt. Fifty-three days later, after Peter's denial, oath, cursing, and finally bitter tears, he preached one of the greatest messages ever on the Day of Pentecost and 3,000 souls were saved (Acts 2:14-41). Peter repented, was restored and reinstated, and God used him mightily despite his failures. That's the power of God's grace!

JOSEPH OF ARIMATHAEA AND NICODEMUS

Let's go back to Jesus being taken before Caiaphas, the High Priest. That evening, Jesus was arrested at night which was against Jewish law. The trial of Jesus before the Sanhedrin Court following His arrest at night is considered to be the most infamous, unjust trial in world history. The Sanhedrin illegally violated the Torah during the trial. Jesus was tried without all the Sanhedrin members being present. Two of the Sanhedrin members who supported Jesus were present—Joseph of Arimathaea and Nicodemus. Joseph was the wealthy man who assumed responsibility for the burial of Jesus after His crucifixion by providing his own tomb. Nicodemus, remember, was a ruler of the Jews who first visited Jesus by night to discuss being born again (John 3:1-2). They both collaborated to bury the body of Jesus, *"And after this Joseph of Arimathaea, being a disciple of Jesus, but secretly for fear of the Jews, besought Pilate that he might take away the body of Jesus: and Pilate gave him leave. He came therefore, and took the body of Jesus. And there came also Nicodemus, which at the first came to Jesus by night, and brought a mixture of myrrh and aloes, about an hundred pound weight. Then took they the body of Jesus, and wound it in linen clothes with the spices, as the manner of the Jews is to bury. Now in the place where he was crucified there was a garden; and in the garden a new sepulchre, wherein was never man yet laid. There laid they Jesus therefore because of the Jews' preparation day; for the sepulchre was nigh at hand"* (John 19:38-42).

Jesus' burial was actually a burial fit for a king. Notice the similar details recorded of King Asa's burial in 2 Chronicles 16:14, *"And they buried him in his own sepulchres, which he had made for himself in the city of David, and laid him in the bed which was filled with sweet odours and divers kinds of spices prepared by the apothecaries' art: and they made a very great burning for him."* Mary had also anointed Jesus for His burial with extravagant, expensive oil. *"Then took Mary a pound of ointment of spikenard, very costly, and anointed the feet of Jesus, and wiped his feet with her hair: and the house was filled with the odour of the ointment"* (John 12:3). The large amount of spices used in verse 39 obviously expressed their deep love for Jesus, just like the extravagant gift Mary had used for His burial earlier.

> *Jesus' burial was actually a burial fit for a king.*

Royalty were usually buried in a garden. *"And Manasseh slept with his fathers, and was buried in the garden of his own house, in the garden of Uzza: and Amon his son reigned in his stead"* (2 Kings 21:18). Here is another example, *"After him repaired Nehemiah the son of Azbuk, the ruler of the half part of Bethzur, unto the place over against the sepulchres of David, and to the pool that was made, and unto the house of the mighty"* (Nehemiah 3:16). Even in His death Jesus was recognized as King. A new tomb was a token of honor given to a king. Jesus was not buried as some in an ancestral tomb. Joseph and Nicodemus came out of hiding to bury Jesus. Just maybe they were in the upper room on Pentecost to receive the outpouring of the Spirit. They could have been part of the reason many priests believed in Jesus. *"And the word of God increased; and the number of the disciples multiplied in Jerusalem greatly; and* **a great company of the priests were obedient to the faith***"* (Acts 6:7).

It is possible that their influence affected the trail of Paul in Acts 22:30: *"On the morrow, because he would have known the certainty wherefore he was accused of the Jews, he loosed him from his bands, and commanded the chief priests and all their council to appear, and brought Paul down, and set him before them."* Acts 23:1-9 gives the account of Paul standing before the Sanhedrin Court, *"And Paul, earnestly beholding the council, said, Men and brethren, I have lived in all good conscience before God until this day. And the high priest Ananias commanded them that stood by him to smite him on the mouth. Then said Paul unto him, God shall smite thee, thou whited wall: for sittest thou to judge me after the law, and commandest me to be smitten contrary to the law? And they that stood by said, Revilest thou God's high priest? Then said Paul, I wist not, brethren, that he was the high priest: for it is written, Thou shalt not speak evil of the ruler of thy people. But when Paul perceived that the one part were Sadducees, and the other Pharisees, he cried out in the council, Men and brethren, I am a Pharisee, the son of a Pharisee: of the hope and resurrection of the dead I am called in question. And when he had so said, there arose a dissension between the Pharisees and the Sadducees: and the multitude was divided. For the Sadducees say that there is no resurrection, neither angel, nor spirit: but the Pharisees confess both. And there arose a great cry: and the scribes that were of the Pharisees' part arose, and strove, saying, We find no evil in this man: but if a spirit or an angel hath spoken to him, let us not fight against God."* The Sadducees didn't believe in the resurrection, but the Pharisees did. Paul cried out to the Pharisees. What if Joseph of Arimathaea or Nicodemus had shared with them the resurrection of Jesus? It's a possibility, I can't prove it, but I believe it and there have been stories written about their influence and involvement in the early church.

JESUS' TRIAL BEFORE PILATE AND HEROD

Let's go back to John 18. Then they led Jesus before Pontius Pilate. *"Then led they Jesus from Caiaphas unto the hall of judgment: and it was early; and they themselves went not into the judgment hall, lest they should be defiled; but that they might eat the Passover"* (John 18:28). They didn't enter the judgment hall lest they should be defiled and banned from celebrating Passover. Then Pilate began to examine Jesus, *"Pilate then went out unto them, and said, What accusation bring ye against this man? They answered and said unto him, If he were not a malefactor, we would not have delivered him up unto thee. Then said Pilate unto them, Take ye him, and judge him according to your law. The Jews therefore said unto him, It is not lawful for us to put any man to death: That the saying of Jesus might be fulfilled, which he spake, signifying what death he should die"* (John 18:29-32).

In this trial before Pontius Pilate, the kingdom of God faces up against the kingdom of Caesar. Look at verse 30. The Jewish religious leaders did not want Pontius Pilate to be a judge, but the executor of the sentence they had already passed on Jesus. The death sentence they passed was totally illegal. They were saying we condemned Him already; you carry out the sentence. In verse 31, Pontius Pilate told them to handle the matter themselves. They knew they shouldn't bring the charges of blasphemy before Pontius Pilate. When Pilate heard Jesus was from Galilee, he sent him to Herod to deal with, *"And the whole multitude of them arose, and led him unto Pilate. And they began to accuse him, saying, We found this fellow perverting the nation, and forbidding to give tribute to Caesar, saying that he himself is Christ a King. And Pilate asked him, saying, Art thou the King of the Jews? And he answered him and said, Thou sayest it. Then said Pilate to the chief priests and to the people, I find no fault in this man. And they were the more fierce, saying, He stirreth up the people, teaching throughout all Jewry, beginning from Galilee to this place.* **When Pilate heard of Galilee, he asked whether the man were a Galilaean. And as soon as he knew that he belonged unto Herod's jurisdiction, he sent him to Herod**, *who himself also was at Jerusalem at that time.*

And when Herod saw Jesus, he was exceeding glad: for he was desirous to see him of a long season, because he had heard many things of him; and he hoped to have seen some miracle done by him. Then he questioned with him in many words; but he answered him nothing. And the chief priests and scribes stood and vehemently accused him. And Herod with his men of war set him at nought, and mocked him, and arrayed him in a gorgeous robe, and sent him again to Pilate. And the same day Pilate and Herod were made friends together: for before they were at enmity between themselves" (Luke 23:1-12). Both Herod and Pilate found no fault in Jesus.

Then, Herod sent Jesus back to Pilate. *"Then Pilate entered into the judgment hall again, and called Jesus, and said unto him, Art thou the King of the Jews? Jesus answered him, Sayest thou this thing of thyself, or did others tell it thee of me? Pilate answered, Am I a Jew? Thine own nation and the chief priests have delivered thee unto me: what hast thou done? Jesus answered, My kingdom is not of this world: if my kingdom were of this world, then would my servants fight, that I should not be delivered to the Jews: but now is my kingdom not from hence. Pilate therefore said unto him, Art thou a king then? Jesus answered, Thou sayest that I am a king. To this end was I born, and for this cause came I into the world, that I should bear witness unto the truth. Every one that is of the truth heareth my voice. Pilate saith unto him, What is truth? And when he had said this, he went out again unto the Jews, and saith unto them, I find in him no fault at all. But ye have a custom, that I should release unto you one at the passover: will ye therefore that I release unto you the King of the Jews? Then cried they all again, saying, Not this man, but Barabbas. Now*

Barabbas was a robber" (John 18:33-40). In verse 33, Pilate asked Jesus, "Art thou the King of the Jews?" He looked at Jesus and asked, I believe, in a mocking way.

In verse 34, Jesus answers Pilate in so many words, "Are you saying this on your own initiative or because of what others have said about me?" In verse 35, Pilate answered by saying, "Am I a Jew?" That was another way of saying, "I am not a Jew." It was your own nation and leaders that delivered you to me. Then Pilate asked, "what hast thou done?" In verse 36, Jesus does not answer Pilate's question, but instead begins to elaborate on His kingdom. Jesus made it clear to Pontius Pilate that His kingdom is not a political, earthly kingdom, but a spiritual, heavenly kingdom. In verse 37, Pilate asked, "Art thou a King then?" Pilate saw a man who outwardly did not look like a king. To this Jesus replied, "Thou sayest that I am a King" or "you say correctly that I am a King." Jesus made it clear why He was born and came into this world by referring to His pre-existence and deity. Jesus was saying, "I am going to establish my kingdom here on earth but not by military force, but by bearing witness to the truth."

Jesus sets up His kingdom by declaring the truth by the help of the Spirit of Truth. *"Howbeit when he, **the Spirit of truth**, is come, he will guide you into all truth: for he shall not speak of himself; but whatsoever he shall hear, that shall he speak: and he will shew you things to come"* (John 16:13). He will guide you into the kingdom of truth. In verse 38, Pilate asked, "What is truth"? Then he went out to the mob and told them, "I find no fault at all." The lamb of God was examined again with no fault found. However, the crowd rejected Jesus and chose to free Barabbas instead. Pilate had hoped they would spare Jesus. *"But the chief priests and elders persuaded the multitude that they* *should ask Barabbas, and destroy Jesus"* (Matthew 27:20). Mark 15:11 agrees, *"But the chief priests moved the people, that he should rather release Barabbas unto them."* The crowd had to be paid off or at least influenced by the chief priests and elders. The mob chose Barabbas whose name means "son of the father." They chose the one who was the son of their Father (the devil) instead of choosing the true Son of God the Father (Jesus). Barabbas was accused of at least three crimes: theft, insurrection, and murder. *"And there was one named Barabbas, which lay bound with them that had made insurrection with him,* **who had committed murder in the insurrection***"* (Mark 15:7). Jesus died in Barabbas's place. He didn't only take Barabbas' place, but He took our place also. *"But God commendeth his love toward us, in that, while we were yet sinners,* **Christ died for us***"* (Romans 5:8).

Oh, how He loves you and me!

CHAPTER 7

THE CRUCIFIXION OF JESUS
(John 19)

John chapter 19 in the New Testament describes the crucifixion of our Lord Jesus Christ. I cannot read this chapter without my eyes filling with tears. Pilate's wife had a dream about Jesus and warned him not to do anything against this "just man." *"When he was set down on the judgment seat, his wife sent unto him, saying, Have thou nothing to do with that just man: for I have suffered many things this day in a dream because of him"* (Matthew 27:19). Pilate realized he could not convince the religious leaders of anything good concerning Jesus. *"When Pilate saw that he could prevail nothing, but that rather a tumult was made, he took water, and washed his hands before the multitude, saying, I am innocent of the blood of this just person: see ye to it. Then answered all the people, and said, His blood be on us, and on our children"* (Matthew 27:24-25). As John 19 opens, Pilate decided to try one more time: *"Then Pilate therefore took Jesus, and scourged him. And the soldiers platted a crown of thorns, and put it on his head, and they put on him a purple robe, And said, Hail, King of the Jews! and they smote him with their hands. Pilate therefore went forth again, and saith unto them, Behold, I bring him forth to you, that ye may know that I find no fault in him. Then came Jesus forth, wearing the crown of thorns, and the purple robe. And Pilate saith unto them, Behold the man!"* (John 19:1-5) These verses deal with the scourging of Jesus, the crown of thorns on His head, and the physical abuse inflicted by Pontius Pilate's soldiers.

First, let us take a look at the scourging of Jesus. Mark 15:15 records, *"And so Pilate, willing to content the people, released Barabbas unto them, and delivered Jesus,* **when he had scourged him***, to be crucified."* Matthews 27:26 reads, *"Then released he Barabbas unto them: and* **when he had scourged Jesus***, he delivered him to be crucified."* He was ordered to receive forty stripes save one. The limitation of forty stripes comes from Deuteronomy 25:3—*"****Forty stripes he may give him****,* ***and not exceed****: lest, if he should exceed, and beat him above these with many stripes, then thy brother should seem vile unto thee."* It is said they would stop at thirty-nine just in case they miscounted one and might go over the limit. According to Jewish law, if the flogger went over, he himself would be flogged for breaking God's law. However, the Romans were not bound by Jewish law. So, they could beat a prisoner even more if they chose to. The first century Jewish historian, Josephus, recorded that there were thirteen stripes on the chest, thirteen on the back, and thirteen on the side, or a total of thirty-nine lacerations. When a decision was made to scourge someone, they would first strip the victim completely naked so his entire flesh would be exposed to the torturer's whip. Then they would bind him to a whipping post.

The Romans were experts at scourging. They took great delight in precisely performing this brutal act; the torture was unimaginable. The whip consisted of a short wooden handle with several straps of leather eighteen to twenty-four inches long. The ends of the strips of leather contained sharp pieces of metal, glass, and lamb bone. This sadistic instrument of torture would cut deep into the skin and tissue tearing into the underlying skeletal muscles and ripping away the flesh. Needless to say, severe scourging was extremely painful. Isaiah prophesied of Jesus, *"As many were astonied at thee;* **his visage was so marred more than any man***, and his form more than the sons of men"* (Isaiah 52:14). Jesus looked more like a piece of meat in a butcher shop than a human being.

Pilate may have thought he could help Jesus by sparing His life and satisfying the mob. John 19:2 tells how they mocked Jesus' claim to be a king, *"And the soldiers platted a* **crown of thorns***, and put it on his head, and they put on him a purple robe."* Why did they use a crown of thorns? Genesis 3:17-19 indicates that thorns were a symbol of the curse of sin, *"And unto Adam he said, Because thou hast hearkened unto the voice of thy wife, and hast eaten of the tree, of which I commanded thee, saying, Thou shalt not eat of it:* **cursed is the ground for thy sake***; in sorrow shalt thou eat of it all the days of thy life;* **Thorns also and thistles shall it bring forth to thee***; and thou shalt eat the herb of the field; In the sweat of thy face shalt thou eat bread, till thou return unto the ground; for out of it wast thou taken: for dust thou art, and unto dust shalt thou return."* Adam and Eve disobeyed God's command and sinned, this brought evil and a curse upon humanity and upon the ground. Because of their disobedience, there were thorns, where they hadn't been any before. The soldiers unknowingly took an object of the curse (thorns) and platted a crown for Jesus to wear. They placed it on the head of Jesus, the One who would deliver us from the curse of sin and death.

The Apostle Paul also had to battle with a thorn in the flesh in 2 Corinthians 12:7-9, *"And lest I should be exalted above measure through the abundance of the revelations,* **there was given to me a thorn in the flesh, the messenger of Satan to buffet me***, lest I should be exalted above measure. For this thing I besought the Lord thrice, that it might depart from me. And he said unto me, My grace is sufficient for thee: for my strength is made perfect in weakness. Most gladly therefore will I rather glory in my infirmities, that the power of Christ may rest upon me."* As mentioned earlier, Jesus started to drink the cup of wrath in the Garden of Gethsemane, just before His arrest. He asked the Father three times, *"My Father, if it is possible, let this cup pass from me."* Jesus was not just expected to sip on it, but to drink all of it. Remember, Jesus did His suffering in the flesh for us.

In 2 Corinthians 12:10-12, Paul wrote about his thorn in the flesh, *"Therefore I take pleasure in infirmities, in reproaches, in necessities, in persecutions, in distresses for Christ's sake: for when I am weak, then am I strong. I am become a fool in glorying; ye have compelled me: for I ought to have been commended of you: for in nothing am I behind the very chiefest apostles, though I be nothing. Truly the signs of an apostle were wrought among you in all patience, in signs, and wonders, and mighty deeds."* How many times did Paul beseech the Lord to remove his thorn in the flesh? He prayed three times that it might depart or be removed from Him. The Lord told him, *"My grace is sufficient for thee."* Look at the next few verses. Paul went through some of the same things Christ went through. I am convinced Paul's thorn was the cup of the wrath, his cup of suffering. He said the thorn was a messenger of Satan sent to buffet him. To "buffet" means "to strike repeatedly as waves would buffet the shore." Before Jesus received the crown of thorns, He was beaten with many stripes. I wept before the Lord as I saw the parallels between Paul's and Jesus' suffering.

Next, I want you to consider Matthew 20:17-19, *"And Jesus going up to Jerusalem took the twelve disciples apart in the way, and said unto them, Behold, we go up to Jerusalem; and the Son of man shall be betrayed unto the chief priests and unto the scribes, and they shall condemn him to death, And shall deliver him to the Gentiles to mock, and to scourge, and to crucify him: and the third day he shall rise again."* Jesus entered Jerusalem six days before the Passover. As they went, He told His disciples how He would be betrayed and condemned to death. He also told them how he would be mocked, scourged, crucified, and raised on the third day. Remember what James' and John's mother ask Jesus concerning her son's position in the kingdom of God? Now look at Jesus' response, *"But Jesus answered and said, Ye know not what ye ask. Are ye able to drink of the cup that I shall drink of, and to be baptized with the baptism that I am baptized with? They say unto him, We are able. And he saith unto them, Ye shall drink indeed of my cup, and be baptized with the baptism that I am baptized with: but to sit on my right hand, and on my left, is not mine to give, but it shall be given to them for whom it is prepared of my Father"* (Matthew 20:22-23).

In what way did they drink the same cup? Jesus was talking about a cup and baptism of suffering. Herod had James killed with the sword (Acts 12:2). James was the first of the disciples to be martyred. John wrote about his persecution in Revelations 1:9, *"I John, who also am your brother, and **companion in tribulation**, and in the* *kingdom and patience of Jesus Christ, was in the isle that is called Patmos, for the word of God, and for the testimony of Jesus Christ."* Foxe's Book of Martyrs records that John survived being cast into a large vessel filled with boiling oil that did not harm him. Some say that John walked on top of the oil. Once source said that John found the oil to be like a hot, refreshing bath. He was forced to drink poison before being exiled to Patmos, a rock quarry island where prisoners were sent to work themselves to death. So, all the original apostles died a violent martyr's death, except for John. Jesus seemed to predict this in John 21:18-22. John definitely drank from that same cup of suffering. Ask yourself, "Am I willing to drink of the same cup and be baptized with the same baptism as Christ?"

"But we see Jesus, who was made a little lower than the angels for the suffering of death, crowned with glory and honour; that he by the grace of God should taste death for every man" (Hebrew 2:9). For our sickness He was scourged that we might be healed. It was our sin and sinful thoughts that pierced the head of Jesus. Adam and Eve were to dress the Garden of Eden and keep it. Thorns grew as a result of the curse caused by man's disobedience (Genesis 3:17-18). Everything was prophesied concerning Jesus beforehand. What happened to Abraham and Isaac on Mount Moriah was a type and shadow of Christ's suffering on the cross. *"And Abraham lifted up his eyes, and looked, and behold behind him* **a ram caught in a thicket by his horns***: and Abraham went and took the ram, and offered him up for a burnt offering*

> What happened to Abraham and Isaac on Mount Moriah was a type and shadow of Christ's suffering on the cross.

in the stead of his son" (Genesis 22:13). Abraham assured Isaac, "God will provide HIMSELF A LAMB for a burnt offering." CHRIST HIMSELF, as our substitute, was crowned with thorns (a symbol of the curse of sin) just like the ram caught in the thicket by his horns.

THE SIGNIFICANCE OF THE PURPLE ROBE

What is the significance of the purple robe? *"And Herod with his men of war set him at nought, and mocked him, and **arrayed him in a gorgeous robe**, and sent him again to Pilate"* (Luke 23:11). *"And they stripped him, and **put on him a scarlet robe**"* (Matthew 27:28). John 19:5 says it was a "purple robe." It was a gorgeously dyed robe. Think about this, the only entrance to the Tabernacle faced east and there was a curtain colored blue on one side and red on the other side. The colors blended in the middle to make purple. Someone said the curtain represented God and man meeting together. Blue represents heaven or deity. Red is for the earth or mankind. Adam can be translated "red man." The two being blended together make purple, representing God and man. Purple is also the color of royalty which speaks of the kingship of Christ. By His death, Jesus became the curtain or the door, our only access to the Father as He stated in John 14:6, *"Jesus saith unto him, **I am the way**, the truth, and the life: no man cometh unto the Father, but by me."* In John 10:7-9, Jesus claimed, *"Verily, verily, I say unto you, **I am the door of the sheep**. All that ever came before me are thieves and robbers: but the sheep did not hear them. **I am the door**: by me if any man enter in, he shall be saved, and shall go in and out, and find pasture."*

The soldiers mockingly worshipped Him; these acts were so horrific. *"And said, Hail, King of the Jews! and they smote him with their hands"* (John 19:3) Matthew 27:30 indicates, *"They spit upon him, and took the reed, and smote him on the head."* Mark 15:19 informs us, *"They smote him on the head with a reed, and did spit upon him, and bowing their knees worshipped him."* Jesus was our perfect example of turning the other cheek because He was silent before His accusers and He did not call down the angels to intervene from heaven. *"Thinkest thou that I cannot now pray to my Father, and he shall presently give me **more than twelve legions of angels**?"* (Matthew 26:53). A legion of angels can be compared to a Roman legion at that time which consisted of 6,000 soldiers. Jesus mentioned twelve legions of angels. That would have been 72,000 angels. From the beginning of this conflict between the kingdom of God and the kingdom of this world which started in the Garden of Gethsemane, the angels were at Jesus command. *"And there appeared **an angel** unto him from heaven, strengthening him"* (Luke 22:43). When Jesus said, "I am He," in the Garden of Gethsemane, these angels moved at His word and knocked all of the soldiers who came to arrest Him backwards to the ground.

*"Pilate therefore went forth again, and saith unto them, Behold, I bring him forth to you, that ye may know that I find no fault in him. Then came Jesus forth, wearing the crown of thorns, and **the purple robe**. And Pilate saith unto them, Behold the man! When the chief priests therefore and officers saw him, they cried out, saying, Crucify him, crucify him. Pilate saith unto them, Take ye him, and crucify him: for I find no fault in him"* (John 19:4-6). Pilate took Jesus before the people hoping they would be pleased after seeing Jesus in such a beaten condition. Pilate found no fault in Jesus again. Pilate allowed

all this to be done to Jesus whom he had judged innocent to gratify the Jews. Notice Pilate's words in verse 5, "Behold the man." He was saying, "This is a just man, a perfect man with no fault at all." Remember, Jesus bore all this suffering as a man, not as God. Then Pilate pronounced Jesus was innocent for the third time of all accusations charged against Him. He told the religious Jews to take Him and crucify Him. *"The Jews answered him, We have a law, and by our law he ought to die, because he made himself the Son of God. When Pilate therefore heard that saying, he was the more afraid"* (John 19:7-8).

In these verses, the Jews revealed what all this was really about. Look at these two verses: *"For he knew that the chief priests had delivered him for envy"* (Mark 15:10). *"For he knew that for envy they had delivered him"* (Matthew 27:18). Pilate knew their whole plot to kill Jesus was motivated by envy. Always remember this saying, "Honor for someone will expose envy in the dishonorable." Envy here is a lust for the praises of the crowd. Jesus Christ's ministry was a threat to the religious leaders. The hostility toward Jesus increased after He raised Lazarus from the dead. *"And he that was dead came forth, bound hand and foot with graveclothes: and his face was bound about with a napkin. Jesus saith unto them, Loose him, and let him go. Then many of the Jews which came to Mary, and had seen the things which Jesus did, believed on him. But some of them went their ways to the Pharisees, and told them what things Jesus had done. Then gathered the chief priests and the Pharisees a council, and said, What do we? for this man doeth many miracles.* **If we let him thus alone, all men will believe on him: and the Romans shall come and take away both our place and nation"** (John 11:44-48). The religious leaders were afraid of losing their position and power.

Now, let us read further, *"And one of them, named Caiaphas, being the high priest that same year, said unto them, Ye know nothing at all, Nor consider that it is expedient for us, that one man should die for the people, and that the whole nation perish not. And this spake he not of himself: but being high priest that year, he prophesied that Jesus should die for that nation; And not for that nation only, but that also he should gather together in one the children of God that were scattered abroad. Then from that day forth they took counsel together for to put him to death"* (John 11:49-53). Here Jesus' enemy (Caiaphas) prophesied that He would die for the nation of Israel and gather them together that are scattered throughout the world. Wow! How amazing is our God in what and who He can use! *"Jesus therefore walked no more openly among the Jews; but went thence unto a country near to the wilderness, into a city called Ephraim, and there continued with his disciples"* (John 11:54).

All the Pharisees and leaders of that day could see, they were losing the crowds, *"The Pharisees therefore said among themselves, Perceive ye how ye prevail nothing?* **Behold, the world is gone after him**" (John 12:19). Caiaphas didn't realize he was prophesying. Was his reasoning really good for the people? As we would say in North Carolina, "Bologna!" By saying this, he was trying to hide his envy. Even by Caiaphas' and the religious leader's envy, they were helping to fulfill God's plan. All this was ordained in the foreknowledge God. *"Him, being delivered by the determinate counsel and* **foreknowledge of God**, *ye have taken, and by wicked hands have crucified and slain"* (Acts 2:23). *"For of a truth against thy holy child Jesus, whom thou hast anointed, both Herod, and Pontius*

Pilate, with the Gentiles, and the people of Israel, were gathered together, for to do whatsoever thy hand and thy counsel determined before to be done" (Acts 4:27-28).

Let's move on to John 19:8-11, *"When Pilate therefore heard that saying, he was the more afraid; And went again into the judgment hall, and saith unto Jesus, Whence art thou? But Jesus gave him no answer. Then saith Pilate unto him, Speakest thou not unto me? knowest thou not that I have power to crucify thee, and have power to release thee? Jesus answered, Thou couldest have no power at all against me, except it were given thee from above: therefore he that delivered me unto thee hath the greater sin."* Because of his wife's dream and how Jesus responded to all His suffering, Pilate was afraid. He must have been wondering who this Jesus really was. Was He sent from God? At this point Pilate became even more afraid. He had heard Jesus claim a kingdom which was not of this world. *"When he was set down on the judgment seat, his wife sent unto him, saying, Have thou nothing to do with that just man: for I have suffered many things this day in a dream because of him"* (Matthew 27:19).

Pilate was already fearful of shedding innocent blood. Pilate was probably questioning himself, "What if Jesus is Divine and the Son of God?" A question that all must answer. In verse nine, Pilate asked Jesus, "Whence art thou?" or "where did you come from?" Pilate suspected Jesus was Divine at this point and that He came from God. Jesus gave Pilate no answer. Pilate was shocked by the silence of Jesus. Look at his reply, *"Then saith Pilate unto him, Speakest thou not unto me? knowest thou not that I have power to crucify thee, and have power to release thee? Jesus answered, Thou couldest have no power at all against me, except it were given thee from above:*

therefore he that delivered me unto thee hath the greater sin" (John 19:10-11). In this statement Jesus is making it clear to Pilate that He was from above and that Pilate had no power over Him. Look at the last statement in this verse, "He that delivered me unto you hath the greater sin." Jesus was relieving Pilate from his self-condemnation here. He said, it is not you, Pilate, it is the High Priest and his evil council that is responsible.

THE PLACE CALLED "THE PAVEMENT"

Now, let's read John 19:12-13, *"And from thenceforth Pilate sought to release him: but the Jews cried out, saying, If thou let this man go, thou art not Caesar's friend: whosoever maketh himself a king speaketh against Caesar. When Pilate therefore heard that saying, he brought Jesus forth, and sat down in the judgment seat in a place that is called* **the Pavement***, but in the Hebrew, Gabbatha."* Pilate sought to release Jesus again. Remember this was not the first time. *"But ye have a custom, that I should release unto you one at the passover: will ye therefore that I release unto you the King of the Jews?"* (John 18:39). Look at the answer of the religious Jews in verse 12, *"If thou let this man go, thou art not Caesar's friend."* They were in essence saying if you let Jesus go, you are not loyal to the Emperor Caesar. Pilate knew releasing Jesus would mean political trouble for him.

When Pilate heard this, he brought Jesus out to a place called the pavement or in Hebrew *"Gabbatha."* Pilate's fearful heart couldn't take it anymore. The pavement was also mentioned in 2 Chronicles 7:3, *"And when all the children of Israel saw how the fire came down, and the glory of the Lord upon the house, they bowed themselves with their faces to the ground upon* **the pavement***,* *and worshipped, and praised the Lord, saying, For he is good; for his mercy endureth for ever."* When I was on one of my many trips to Israel, a tour guide explained that Pilate took Jesus to the same place where the people in 2 Chronicles 7:3 *"bowed themselves with their faces to the ground, saying, He is good, and his mercy endureth forever."* Pilate must have been hoping they would realize Jesus was good and would show Him great mercy. In this place, Jesus obtained mercy for us. Everything and every place as Jesus drank the cup of wrath had a purpose and meaning for us.

Next, we move to John 19:14-15, *"And it was the preparation of the passover, and about the sixth hour: and he saith unto the Jews, Behold your King! But they cried out, Away with him, away with him, crucify him. Pilate said unto them, Shall I crucify your King? The chief priests answered, We have no king but Caesar."* In verse fourteen, it says, "about the sixth hour," which is 12:00 noon, but Mark 15:25 records that it was the third hour when they crucified him. The word "about" is very important here to clarify what time it was. By putting these verses together, we know it occurred between nine o'clock and twelve noon. In verse fifteen above, Pilate proclaimed Jesus as "King." It was not in a mocking way this time. Pilate was finally convinced for himself Jesus was King of the Jews. Jesus was referred to as King of the Jews on several occasions during His life. One was at His birth, *"Now when Jesus was born in Bethlehem of Judaea in the days of Herod the king, behold, there came wise men from the east to Jerusalem, Saying,* **Where is he that is born King of the Jews**? *for we have seen his star in the east, and are come to worship him"* (Matthew 2:1-2). This rejection of Jesus is not the first time Israel rejected God as King.

This also happened in the days of Samuel. *"And said unto [Samuel], Behold, thou art old, and thy sons walk not in thy ways: now make us a king to judge us like all the nations. But the thing displeased Samuel, when they said, Give us a king to judge us. And Samuel prayed unto the Lord. And the Lord said unto Samuel, Hearken unto the voice of the people in all that they say unto thee: for they have not rejected thee, but* **they have rejected me***,* **that I should not reign over them***"* (1 Samuel 8:5-7).

Read God's promise to David in 2 Samuel 7:11-17, *"And as since the time that I commanded judges to be over my people Israel, and have caused thee to rest from all thine enemies. Also the Lord telleth thee that he will make thee an house. And when thy days be fulfilled, and thou shalt sleep with thy fathers, I will set up thy seed after thee, which shall proceed out of thy bowels, and I will establish his kingdom. He shall build an house for my name, and I will stablish the throne of his kingdom for ever. I will be his father, and he shall be my son. If he commit iniquity, I will chasten him with the rod of men, and with the stripes of the children of men: But my mercy shall not depart away from him, as I took it from Saul, whom I put away before thee. And thine house and thy kingdom shall be established for ever before thee: thy throne shall be established for ever. According to all these words, and according to all this vision, so did Nathan speak unto David."*

Read verse 14 again, *"I will be his father, and he shall be my son. If he commit iniquity, I will chasten him with the rod of men, and with the stripes of the children of men."* Nathan the prophet was speaking of David's kingdom but also prophetically of Jesus establishing the kingdom of God. Jesus needed no chastisement; it was our chastisement put on Him. Jesus was chastened with the rod of men and with stripes of the children of men as our substitute, *"But he was wounded for our transgressions, he was bruised for our iniquities:* **the chastisement of our peace was upon him**; *and with his stripes we are healed. All we like sheep have gone astray; we have turned every one to his own way; and the Lord hath laid on him the iniquity of us all. He was oppressed, and he was afflicted, yet he opened not his mouth: he is brought as a lamb to the slaughter, and as a sheep before her shearers is dumb, so he openeth not his mouth. He was taken from prison and from judgment: and who shall declare his generation? for he was cut off out of the land of the living: for the transgression of my people was he stricken"* (Isaiah 53:5-8). These following verses express to us the great mercies of the Lord, *"But my mercy shall not depart away from him"* (2 Samuel 7:15). *"O give thanks unto the Lord; for he is good: for his mercy endureth for ever"* (Psalms 136:1). Every verse in Psalms 136 ends with the phrase "His mercy endureth forever." "His mercy endureth forever" means so much more to us now because of what Jesus did for us on the cross.

In John 19:15, the Jews cried out again, *"Away with him, away with Him, crucify Him."* Surprised, Pilate asked them, "Shall I crucify your king?" The chief priest answered, "We have no king but Caesar." This fulfilled the prophecy given in Hosea 3:4, *"***For the children of Israel shall abide many days without a king***, and without a prince, and without a sacrifice, and without an image, and without an ephod, and without teraphim."* They had been without a Jewish king for centuries because they were conquered and occupied by foreign nations. The chief priests hated Caesar but declared him their king, rejecting God as their king the same way they did in Samuel's day. *"If we let him thus alone, all men will believe on him: and the Romans shall come and take away both our place and nation"* (John 11:48). This verse tells us why they rejected Jesus as king. They were afraid of losing their place just as we are afraid to lose our own place when we surrender control of our lives to Christ. This why they declared Caesar as their king. Years later, Nero accused the Christians of burning Rome in 64 AD. The Romans came in and besieged Jerusalem and the Temple area from 66-70 A.D. Evil emperor Nero, who committed suicide in 68 A.D., started the siege and the Emperor Claudius finished it. Jerusalem was destroyed in 70 A.D. just as Jesus prophesied in Matthew 24:2. Tens of thousands of Jews were slain and crucified, and the Temple was burned to the ground.

"Then delivered he him therefore unto them to be crucified. And they took Jesus, and led him away. And he bearing his cross went forth into a place called the place of a skull, which is called in the Hebrew Golgotha: Where they crucified him, and two other with him, on either side one, and Jesus in the midst" (John 19:16-18). The Roman soldiers carried out the execution of Jesus under the direction of the chief priests. When Pilate delivered Him up, he was delivering Him over to the will of His enemies, as is shown in Matthew 27:27-31, *"Then the soldiers of the governor took Jesus into the common hall, and gathered unto him the whole band of soldiers. And they stripped him, and put on him a scarlet robe. And when they had platted a crown of thorns, they put it upon his head, and a reed in his right hand: and they bowed the knee before him, and mocked him, saying, Hail, King of the Jews! And they spit upon him, and took the reed, and smote him on the head. And*

after that they had mocked him, they took the robe off from him, and put his own raiment on him, and led him away to crucify him." After they abused and insulted our Lord, they stripped Jesus naked again. What shame Jesus endured for us. *"Looking unto Jesus the author and finisher of our faith; who for the joy that was set before him* **endured the cross, despising the shame**, *and is set down at the right hand of the throne of God"* (Hebrews 12:2).

At the cross, He was rewriting your story through faith. Jesus despised the shame of being naked before all men. In most pictures of the crucifixion, a loin cloth is seen on the victims out of modesty or decency. The Romans, however, crucified people naked to humiliate them totally and publicly as a warning to others who might rebel. Genesis 2:25 informs us, *"And they were both naked, the man and his wife, and were not ashamed."* Adam and Eve didn't wear clothes before the fall because they were clothed in the glory of God. The first man Adam was created in the image of God. Being created in the righteousness of God, this son of God by his sin was stripped naked and all mankind is born naked because of Adam. But the last Adam (the Lord from heaven) suffered the shame of being stripped naked. But by Jesus' obedience to the cross, our shame is removed, and we are clothed in the righteousness of God.

> *At the cross, He was rewriting your story through faith.*

This is seen in the following verses: *"And to her was granted that she should be arrayed in fine linen, clean and white:* **for the fine linen is the righteousness of saints**" (Revelations 19:8). *"I will greatly rejoice in the Lord, my* soul shall be joyful in my God; for **he hath clothed me with the garments of salvation, he hath covered me with the robe of righteousness,** *as a bridegroom decketh himself with ornaments, and as a bride adorneth herself with her jewels"* (Isaiah 61:10). His promise to us is this—His bride will be clothed with His imparted righteousness.

THE MEANING OF GOLGOTHA AND CALVARY

"And he bearing his cross went forth into a place called the place of a skull, which is called in the Hebrew **Golgotha***"* (John 19:17). Jesus bore His cross and walked to *Golgotha*—the Hebrew word meaning "the place of the skull," which is the same as our English word "Calvary." It is the site where Jesus' crucifixion took place and is mentioned in all four Gospels. It was called the place of the skull either because the hillside resembled the look of a human skull or because actual skulls littered than horrible place of execution. Golgotha was also a place where people were counted in any numbering or census of Israel. *"These were the sons of Levi after the house of their fathers; even the chief of the fathers,* **as they were counted by number of names by their polls***, that did the work for the service of the house of the Lord, from the age of twenty years and upward"* (1 Chronicles 23:24). Numbers 1:2 also refers to this custom, *"***Take ye the sum of all the congregation of the children of Israel***, after their families, by the house of their fathers,* **with the number of their names***,* **every male by their polls***."* The word "polls" in Hebrew is the word *Golgolet*, which means "a skull or a head." By the days of Jesus, *Golgolet* had transformed to *Golgotha*. This is where they counted the people as they entered Jerusalem from the Mount of Olives.

*"Wherefore Jesus also, that he might sanctify the people with his own blood, **suffered without the gate**"* (Hebrews 13:12). Golgotha was outside the gate of Jerusalem.

Numbers 5:1-4 describes how lepers and the unclean were sent outside the camp of Israel, *"And the Lord spake unto Moses, saying, Command the children of Israel, that they **put out of the camp** every leper, and every one that hath an issue, and whosoever is defiled by the dead: Both male and female shall ye put out, **without the camp** shall ye put them; that they defile not their camps, in the midst whereof I dwell. And the children of Israel did so, and **put them out without the camp**."* Those who were ceremonially unclean were sent outside the camp. Churches would be empty if we still did this today. Numbers 15:32-36 details how the law was enforced, and justice was executed outside the camp, *"And while the children of Israel were in the wilderness, they found a man that gathered sticks upon the sabbath day. And they that found him gathering sticks brought him unto Moses and Aaron, and unto all the congregation. And they put him in ward, because it was not declared what should be done to him. And the Lord said unto Moses, The man shall be surely put to death: all the congregation shall stone him with stones without the camp. And all the congregation brought him without the camp, and stoned him with stones, and he died; as the Lord commanded Moses."*

Those who disobeyed God's law were executed outside the camp. This held true in Jesus' day. In Jesus' hometown of Nazareth, they tried to execute Him outside the city because they thought He blasphemed by claiming to be the Anointed One (Christ or Messiah) prophesied in Isaiah 61:1-3. *"And all they in the synagogue, when they heard these things, were filled with wrath. And rose up,* *and **thrust him out of the city**, and led him unto the brow of the hill whereon their city was built, that they might cast him down headlong"* (Luke 4:28-29). This is also demonstrated by the stoning of Stephen in Acts 7:58, *"**And cast him out of the city**, and stoned him: and the witnesses laid down their clothes at a young man's feet, whose name was Saul."* Jesus cleansed us from our uncleanness and disobedience by His precious blood ... outside the city.

John didn't mention the man named Simon of Cyrene, but he is mentioned in the other Gospels. *"And as they came out, they found a man of Cyrene, Simon by name: him they compelled to bear his cross"* (Matthew 27:32). *"And they compel one Simon a Cyrenian, who passed by, coming out of the country, the father of Alexander and Rufus, to bear his cross"* (Mark 15:21). *"And as they led him away, they laid hold upon one Simon, a Cyrenian, coming out of the country, and on him they laid the cross, that he might bear it after Jesus"* (Luke 23:26). Mark mentioned Simon as the father of Alexander and Rufus. Why did Mark think it was important to give us the names of Simon's sons? In that day, many people were named Simon. In fact, there are nine different men named Simon in the New Testament. Mark was distinguishing Simon by his son's names. John was there, but he didn't mention him in his account. Matthew, Luke, and Mark were not there. Did they hear it from Simon's son? Was this the same Rufus mentioned by Paul in Romans 16:13 *"Salute Rufus chosen in the Lord, and his mother and mine."* Was His mother the wife of Simon? Mark mentioned these son's names because people reading this would know who Simon was by His son's name.

Simon means "listening or hearkening." Rufus means "red" while Alexander means "to help or depend." Simon was a type and shadow of all of us who pick up our cross and follow the Lord. *"And he said to them all, If any man will come after me, let him deny himself, and take up his cross daily, and follow me"* (Luke 9:23). Simon is a picture of true discipleship. This may be why the Apostle Paul wrote, *"Who in the days of his flesh, when he had offered up prayers and supplications with strong crying and tears unto him that was able to save him from death, and was heard in that he feared"* (Hebrews 5:7). After all Jesus experienced, He was at the point of death by crucifixion, and was praying not to die before He finished the cup of wrath which He drank for you and me from the garden to the cross.

John 19:18 tells us Jesus was crucified between two criminals, *"Where they crucified him, and two other with him, on either side one, and Jesus in the midst."* This fulfilled Isaiah 53:12 which foretold that Jesus would be numbered with the transgressors, *"Therefore will I divide him a portion with the great, and he shall divide the spoil with the strong; because he hath poured out his soul unto death: and he was **numbered with the transgressors**; and he bare the sin of many, and made intercession for the transgressors."* Not one Word of God can fall to the ground to become meaningless or left unfulfilled. Psalms 119:89 declares, *"For ever, O Lord, thy word is settled in heaven."* What was the reason God ordained this to happen? By doing this, Jesus took our place among the transgressors as our substitute. Jesus, by taking the cup of wrath, was treated as if He had committed every sin ever committed by mankind. The Father was allowing Jesus who knew no sin to become sin for us. *"For he hath made him to be sin for us, who knew no sin; that we might be made the righteousness of God in him"* (2 Corinthians 5:21). This was done for all mankind. God the Father made Jesus become sin, so we might be made the Righteousness of God. Jesus made us righteous, not we ourselves. Jesus purchased righteousness for us on the cross.

Isaiah 64:6 describes our righteousness as filthy garments or rags—*"But we are all as an unclean thing, and all our righteousnesses are as filthy rags; and we all do fade as a leaf; and our iniquities, like the wind, have taken us away."* Ladies, please forgive me for what I am about to write. The phrase "filthy rags" in Hebrew literally means "like soiled rags used for menstruation." I want to point out that when a woman becomes pregnant with a child, she stops bleeding. This is how she knows she is pregnant. In a spiritual sense, when we become pregnant with the Word, we have no use for the filthy rags of our own righteousness. Ephesians 2:1-5 proclaims, *"And you hath he quickened, who were dead in trespasses and sins; Wherein in time past ye walked according to the course of this world, according to the prince of the power of the air, the spirit that now worketh in the children of disobedience: Among whom also we all had our conversation in times past in the lusts of our flesh, fulfilling the desires of the flesh and of the mind; and were by nature the children of wrath, even as others. But God, who is rich in mercy, for his great love wherewith he loved us, Even when we were dead in sins, hath quickened us together with Christ, (by grace ye are saved)."*

John 19:19-22 records, *"And Pilate wrote a title, and put it on the cross. And the writing was JESUS OF NAZARETH THE KING OF THE JEWS. This title then read many of the Jews: for the place where Jesus was crucified was nigh to the city: and it was written in Hebrew, and Greek, and Latin. Then said the chief priests of the Jews to*

Pilate, Write not, The King of the Jews; but that he said, I am King of the Jews. Pilate answered, What I have written I have written." Pilate wrote the title in bold letters just like it is written in the book of John." John wrote that the title "was written in Hebrew, Latin, and Greek," because on the cross, Jesus became the King over all the earth. Those were the three prominent languages spoken in that region of the world at that time. Hundreds of thousands of Jews were in Jerusalem that day to celebrate the Passover and carried the news of this mysterious title all over the then known world.

The cross became a throne that day. His crucifixion is an entrance into the kingdom of God. Paul later wrote, *"If we suffer, we shall also reign with him: if we deny him, he also will deny us"* (2 Timothy 2:12). Luke, the beloved physician, agreed with Paul, *"Confirming the souls of the disciples, and exhorting them to continue in the faith, and that* **we must through much tribulation enter into the kingdom of God***"* (Acts 14:22). Through His suffering and tribulations, we enter in the kingdom of Christ. In John 19:21, they wanted Pilate to add "That He said" to the inscription he put on the cross. They knew King of Jews was a Messianic title reserved only for the Messiah. Pilate was saying that Jesus was their Messiah. In verse twenty-two, Pilate answered, "What I have written, I have written." This statement was an expression for a leader to signify "What I have done can never be undone."

> *"What I have written, I have written. What I have done can never be undone."*

CHAPTER 8

JESUS' SEVEN STATEMENTS FROM THE CROSS

We will now look at the words of Jesus on the cross. Jesus uttered seven short but significant statements from the cross that we will examine.

1. "Father, forgive them; for they know not what they do."

First, let's read Luke 23:34, *"Then said Jesus, **Father, forgive them; for they know not what they do**. And they parted his raiment, and cast lots."* Our Lord Jesus was looking down from the cross. He saw the soldiers who mocked, scourged, and tortured Him and had just nailed Him to the cross. He remembered those who had falsely accused and sentenced an innocent man to death. He remembered Caiaphas and the priests who out of envy handed Him over to Pilate. He remembered Pontius Pilate who knew He was not guilty but gave into the pressure of evil leaders. He remembered the disciples who had fled. He remembered Peter who had denied Him three times. He remembered the crowd that praised Him as He entered Jerusalem, and then just days later demanded, "Crucify Him, Crucify Him!" He also had you and me on His mind, who often forget Him in our lives. His physical suffering was extreme and unimaginable. Jesus never reacted with vengeful anger. His love prevailed and He asked the Father to forgive His own murderers and we whose sin made His death necessary. He had taught His disciples to forgive in the Lord's Prayer—*"And forgive us our debts, as we forgive our debtors"* (Matthew 6:12). Peter asked Jesus, "How many times should we forgive someone?" Jesus answered, "Seventy times seven," or 490 times, an absurdly high number to show that forgiveness should flow freely *"Then came Peter to him, and said, Lord, how oft shall my brother sin against me, and I forgive him? till seven times? Jesus saith unto him, I say not unto thee, Until seven times: but, Until seventy times seven"* (Matthew 18:21-22).

At the last supper, *"And he took the cup, and gave thanks, and gave it to them, saying, Drink ye all of it; For this is my blood of the new testament, which is shed for many for the remission of sins"* (Matthew 26:27-28). Even after the resurrection, He commissioned them to continue to forgive. *"And when he had said this, he breathed on them, and saith unto them, Receive ye the Holy Ghost: Whose soever sins ye remit, they are remitted unto them; and whose soever sins ye retain, they are retained"* (John 20:22-23). Think about this prayer in Luke 23:34, ***"Then said Jesus, Father, forgive them; for they know not what they do."*** In His last hour, Jesus prayed to His Father. In all His suffering, this is unbelievable and brings tears to my eyes as I think deeply about it. We would probably be crying out, "God help me." But Jesus prayed as He always did—unselfishly. Jesus loves us to the very end. At His moment of death, He didn't pray for Himself, but for others. These words were spoken in great love. He did not say, "God Almighty" or "Creator God," but "Father." Jesus cried "Abba" or "Daddy," and if you are in the family, His Spirit leads you. You are not in the family if the Spirit is not in you. If His Spirit is in you, then you can cry "Abba Father" which is a term of endearment and indicates a close, personal relationship. *"For ye have not received the spirit of bondage again to fear; but ye have received the Spirit of adoption, whereby we cry,* **Abba***,* **Father***"* (Romans 8:15). In Galatians 4:6, Paul echoed this idea again, *"And because ye are sons, God hath sent forth the Spirit of his Son into your hearts, crying,* **Abba, Father***."*

Jesus prayed, "forgive them, for they do not know what they are doing." He was praying for the soldiers, Pilate, chief priests, scribes, Pharisees, Sadducees, but also for US. *"For Christ also hath once suffered for sins, the just for the unjust, that he might bring us to God, being put to death in the flesh, but quickened by the Spirit"* (1 Peter 3:18). Our sins made the cross necessary. We are the ones He prayed for to receive forgiveness. Jesus said, "They do not know what they are doing." Paul explained in 1 Corinthians 2:8, *"Which none of the princes of this world knew: for had they known it, they would not have crucified the Lord of glory."*

> *"Forgive them, for they do not know what they are doing."*

Also, look at Peter's words in Acts 3:17, *"And now, brethren, I wot that through ignorance ye did it, as did also your rulers."* The Apostle Paul, who persecuted Christians to their death, did it in ignorance and unbelief. *"Who was before a blasphemer, and a persecutor, and injurious: but I obtained mercy, because* **I did it ignorantly in unbelief***"* (1 Timothy 1:13). Maybe we should take a moment, ask for forgiveness, and forgive others as Jesus did and ask the Lord to reveal what we have done in ignorance and unbelief.

After Jesus asked the Father to forgive them, the soldiers still parted His raiment and cast lots as they gambled for His clothes (Luke 23:34). The mob watched as their rulers derided Jesus even after He had cried out for mercy. *"And the people stood beholding. And the rulers also with them derided him, saying, He saved others; let him save himself, if he be Christ, the chosen of God"* (Luke 23:35). After Jesus asked for their forgiveness, the soldiers still mocked Him offering vinegar as wine, *"And the soldiers also mocked him, coming to him, and offering him vinegar, And saying, If thou be the king of the Jews, save thyself"* (Luke 23:36-37).

2. "Today shalt thou be with me in paradise."

The second statement of Jesus while on the cross was spoken to a repentant, dying thief. Both criminals hanging next to Him blasphemed Jesus at first. Then one had a change of heart when He saw Jesus forgive His own murders. He cried out in desperation for forgiveness, *"And one of the malefactors which were hanged railed on him, saying, If thou be Christ, save thyself and us. But the other answering rebuked him, saying, Dost not thou fear God, seeing thou art in the same condemnation? And we indeed justly; for we receive the due reward of our deeds: but this man hath done nothing amiss. And he said unto Jesus, Lord, remember me when thou comest into thy kingdom"* (Luke 23:39-42). *"And Jesus said unto him, Verily I say unto thee,* **Today shalt thou be with me in paradise***"* (Luke 23:43). It was the criminal on the right that spoke up for Jesus. He spoke to the other criminal saying, "This man has done nothing wrong." One thief rejected Jesus, the other one accepted Jesus. Which one are you? Look at what the thief on the right said in Luke 23:40, *"Dost not thou fear God, seeing thou art in the same condemnation?"* Because of Adam's sin condemnation came on all men. Romans 5:18 declares, *"Therefore as by the offence of one **judgment came upon all men to condemnation**; even so by the righteousness of one the free gift came upon all men unto justification of life."* Jesus took our condemnation for us. ***"There is therefore now no condemnation to them which are in Christ Jesus**, who walk not after the flesh, but after the Spirit. For the law of the Spirit of life in Christ Jesus hath made me free from the law of sin and death. For what the law could not do, in that it was weak through the flesh, God sending his own Son in the likeness of sinful flesh, and for sin, condemned sin in the flesh: That the righteousness of the law might be fulfilled in us, who walk not after the flesh, but after the Spirit"* (Romans 8:1-4). So, we see that condemnation is done away in Christ Jesus.

That thief, though crucified on earth for his crimes, now walks a free man in heaven. Jesus promised him a place in paradise. The word translated "paradise" means a park or garden (as in the Garden of Eden). Nelson's Illustrated Bible Dictionary says, it implies "a place of exceptional happiness and delight and is a descriptive name for heaven. Various commentators have pointed out that when a Persian king wished to bestow upon one of his subjects a special honor, he made him a 'companion of the garden.' The subject was chosen to walk in the king's garden as a special friend and companion of the king. Thus, Jesus promised the thief that he would be a companion of the King of kings, walking with Christ in the garden of heaven." What Jesus said to that thief is a message of hope to us all. If Jesus saved a desperate, dying thief, He will save us too. Thank God, there is no sin too big for the blood of Jesus to handle!

3. "Woman, behold thy son … behold thy mother."

Now we move to His third statement on the cross, *"When Jesus therefore saw his mother, and the disciple standing by, whom he loved, he saith unto his mother,* **Woman, behold thy son***! Then saith he to the disciple,* **Behold thy mother***! And from that hour that disciple took her unto his own home"* (John 19:26-27). Jesus and Mary had probably always been together from the time she became pregnant with Him up to the beginning of His ministry. Now, at the foot of the cross, she was with Him again watching Him suffer. Jesus saw His mother, but He also saw John and He spoke to His mother saying, *"Woman, behold thy son."*

Please understand in that day using the word "woman" referring to a female was a very respectful way to address her, just as we would say madam or lady. (Remember, Jesus also addressed His mother as "woman" at the wedding in Cana where He performed His first miracle in John 2:4). Since Jesus was the oldest son, it was His responsibility to care for His mother. Jesus made provision for His mother by charging John to take care of her. You might ask, "why not His brothers?" For one thing, they were not yet believers and where were her other sons during the time of her greatest sorrow? They were probably hiding in fear for their own lives. But John was there. He was the only male disciple to follow Jesus to the cross. John 7:5 indicates, *"For neither did his brethren believe in him.* Matthew 13:55 informs us that Jesus had four brothers, *"Is not this the carpenter's son? is not his mother called Mary? and his brethren, James, and Joses, and Simon, and Judas?"* James came to believe in the Lord after seeing Him alive after the resurrection. *"After that, he was seen of above five hundred brethren at once; of whom the greater part remain unto this present, but some are fallen asleep. After that, he was seen of James; then of all the apostles. And last of all he was seen of me also, as of one born out of due time"* (1 Corinthians 15:6-8). James became the leader of the church at Jerusalem. Jesus also had at least two sisters (Matthew 13:56, Mark 6:3) and His brothers were among the 120 on the Day of Pentecost (Acts 1:14). Jesus saw His mother at the foot of the cross and had pity on her. Mary was a woman of sorrows and well acquainted with grief. *"And the angel came in unto her, and said, Hail, thou that art highly favoured, the Lord is with thee: blessed art thou among women. And when she saw him, she was troubled at his saying, and cast in her mind what manner of salutation this should be"* (Luke 1:28-29).

The Sword That Pierced Mary's Heart

Here are some of the sorrows of Mary faced as Jesus' mother, she gave birth to Jesus in a cave and laid Him in a manger (a feeding trough for animals), then Herod sought to kill her baby so they had to flee to Egypt, later she was terrified because she couldn't find Jesus in the crowd at age twelve, Her son was despised and rejected of men, plus her other children did not believe in Jesus or believe her until after His resurrection, finally, she witnessed His trial and then watched Him tortured on the cross. Imagine how her soul felt like it was pierced through with a sword. All of this was a fulfillment of Simeon's prophecy given in Luke 2:25-35 when Joseph and Mary took baby Jesus up to the Temple for His dedication, *"And, behold, there was a man in Jerusalem, whose name was Simeon; and the same man was just and devout, waiting for the consolation of Israel: and the Holy Ghost was upon him. And it was revealed unto him by the Holy Ghost, that he should not see death, before he had seen the Lord's Christ. And he came by the Spirit into the temple: and when the parents brought in the child Jesus, to do for him after the custom of the law, Then took he him up in his arms, and blessed God, and said, Lord, now lettest thou thy servant depart in peace, according to thy word: For mine eyes have seen thy salvation, Which thou hast prepared before the face of all people; A light to lighten the Gentiles, and the glory of thy people Israel. And Joseph and his mother marvelled at those things which were spoken of him. And Simeon blessed them, and said unto Mary his mother, Behold, this child is set for the fall and rising again of many in Israel; and for a sign which shall be spoken against; (Yea, **a sword shall pierce through thy own soul also**,) that the thoughts of many hearts may be revealed."* Simeon had been promised that he would not die until he saw the Messiah. The same voice told Simeon to go to the temple that day. Simeon received Jesus in his arms as an infant and spoke of God's salvation for all people, a light to the Gentiles and the glory of Israel. After seeing Jesus, Simeon was ready to die.

Joseph and Mary brought the infant Jesus to the Temple as written in the law of the Lord. They offered a sacrifice according to the law of the Lord. *"Speak unto the children of Israel, saying, If a woman have conceived seed, and born a man child: then she shall be unclean seven days; according to the days of the separation for her infirmity shall she be unclean. And in the eighth day the flesh of his foreskin shall be circumcised. And she shall then continue in the blood of her purifying three and thirty days; she shall touch no hallowed thing, nor come into the sanctuary, until the days of her purifying be fulfilled. But if she bear a maid child, then she shall be unclean two weeks, as in her separation: and she shall continue in the blood of her purifying threescore and six days. And when the days of her purifying are fulfilled, for a son, or for a daughter, she shall bring a lamb of the first year for a burnt offering, and a young pigeon, or a turtledove, for a sin offering, unto the door of the tabernacle of the congregation, unto the priest: Who shall offer it before the Lord, and make an atonement for her; and she shall be cleansed from the issue of her blood. This is the law for her that hath born a male or a female. And if she be not able to bring a lamb, then she shall bring two turtles, or two young pigeons; the one for the burnt offering, and the other for a sin offering: and the priest shall make an atonement for her, and she shall be clean"* (Leviticus 12:2-8).

Anna the prophetess also recognizes Jesus as the Messiah. She spoke about the infant Jesus, *"And she coming in that instant gave thanks likewise unto the Lord, and spake of him to all them that looked for redemption in Jerusalem"* (Luke 2:38). According to Luke, she was eighty-four years old, *"And there was one Anna, a prophetess, the daughter of Phanuel, of the tribe of Aser: she was of a great age, and had lived with an husband seven years from her virginity"* (Luke 2:36). She had no desire to die but was driven to bear witness to what she has seen. Anna the Prophetess was the first woman or man to openly proclaim the good news of the Messiah. Anna was not just visiting the House of God for a day, she was there all the time—*"And she was a widow of about fourscore and four* *years, which **departed not from the temple**, but served God with fastings and prayers night and day"* (Luke 2:37). Anna never left the Temple, but worship God night and day with fasting and prayer. Oh, how the presence and the power of God must have rested upon her.

Gambling for Jesus' Garments

Let's go back to the parting of Jesus' garments. John 19:23-24 describes what happened, *"Then the soldiers, when they had crucified Jesus, took his garments, and made four parts, to every soldier a part; and also his coat: now the coat was without seam, woven from the top throughout. They said therefore among themselves, Let us not rend it, but cast lots for it, whose it shall be: that the scripture might be fulfilled, which saith, They parted my raiment among them, and for my vesture they did cast lots. These things therefore the soldiers did."* Jesus prayed these words as He looked down at those who gambled for His clothes, "Father forgive them." It was a coat without seams, an outer garment. Exodus 39:22-23 gives the details about the High Priest's garment, *"And he made the robe of the ephod of woven work, all of blue. And there was an hole in the midst of the robe, as the hole of an habergeon, with a band round about the hole, that it should not rend."* Aaron, the first High Priest, also had a seamless garment. Jesus, the Great High Priest of His people, had a coat made in a similar manner which probably angered the chief priests even more.

The soldiers gambling for His clothing was the fulfillment of Psalms 22:18, *"They part my garments among them, and cast lots upon my vesture."* They were fighting over His garment which was seamless instead of ripping it and cast lots for it. *"And after that they had mocked him, they took the robe off from him, and put his own raiment on him, and led him away to crucify him"* (Matthew 27:31). They stripped Jesus of all His clothes again at the cross and they gambled for the seamless coat. This tells us they put His own clothes back on Him. Jesus was clothed as He was carrying the cross and now stripped again naked for us. Jesus was stripped that we might be clothed with His righteousness. So, they parted Jesus' clothing, but they cast lots for His seamless coat. The seamless garment would have been the *Tallit* or Prayer Shawl. Seamlessness is a picture of the unity He desires for us. *"And there shall be an hole in the top of it, in the midst thereof: it shall have a binding of woven work round about the hole of it, as it were the hole of an habergeon,* **that it be not rent"** (Exodus 28:32). This verse forbade the tearing of the high priest's clothes. Since Caiaphas, the High Priest, rent his own clothes, he would no longer legally be considered High Priest. *"Then the high priest rent his clothes, saying, He hath spoken blasphemy; what further need have we of witnesses? behold, now ye have heard his blasphemy"* (Matthew 26:65).

Next Matthew, Mark, and Luke recorded the tearing of the veil in the Temple after the death of Jesus on the cross. *"And, behold,* **the veil of the temple was rent in twain from the top to the bottom**; *and the earth did quake, and the rocks rent; And the graves were opened; and many bodies of the saints which slept arose"* (Matthew 27:51-52). *"And the veil of the temple was rent in twain from the top to the bottom"* (Mark 15:38). *"And the sun was darkened, and the veil of the temple was rent in the midst"* (Luke 23:45). The veil, or curtain, in the Temple was torn in two from top to bottom upon the death of Jesus.

All three of the Synoptic Gospels mention the veil of

the Temple which is referring to the innermost curtain. This veil separated the Holy Place and the Holy of Holies. We read about it in Exodus 26:31-33, *"And thou shalt make a vail of blue, and purple, and scarlet, and fine twined linen of cunning work: with cherubims shall it be made: And thou shalt hang it upon four pillars of shittim wood overlaid with gold: their hooks shall be of gold, upon the four sockets of silver. And thou shalt hang up the vail under the taches, that thou mayest bring in thither within the vail the ark of the testimony: and the vail shall divide unto you between the holy place and the most holy."* That curtain symbolized the separation of God and man. Only the high priest could walk through the veil on the annual Day of Atonement to sprinkle the blood of the atoning sacrifice upon the Mercy Seat, the golden lid of the Ark of the Covenant. Sin was unworthy to stand in God's holy presence. The priest had to go through ceremonial cleansing before entering. *"And he said, Thou canst not see my face: for there shall no man see me, and live"* (Exodus 33:20). The Father tore the curtain that separated us from Him at the moment of Jesus' death.

Hebrews 10:19-22 describes the access we now have to God's presence, *"**Having therefore, brethren, boldness to enter into the holiest by the blood of Jesus,** By a new and living way, which he hath consecrated for us, through the veil, that is to say, his flesh; And having an high priest over the house of God; Let us draw near with a true heart in full assurance of faith, having our hearts sprinkled from an evil conscience, and our bodies washed with pure water."* Jesus made a way back to God. Jesus reconciled us back to God through His death. *"For if, when we were enemies, we were reconciled to God by the death of his Son, much more, being reconciled, we shall be saved by* *his life"* (Romans 5:10). We are saved by His resurrection. We have confidence to enter the most Holy of Holies by the blood of Jesus. Through Jesus we have unlimited access to the Father, no more separation. We are no longer "dead" but now we are "alive!"

Many believe the Ark of the Covenant that contained the Ten Commandments was hidden in a cave underneath Calvary. By Solomon's time, when the Ark was moved from the Tabernacle of David into the Temple, *"**There was nothing in the ark save the two tables of stone**, which Moses put there at Horeb, when the Lord made a covenant with the children of Israel, when they came out of the land of Egypt"* (1 King 8:9). *"Jesus, when he had cried again with a loud voice, yielded up the ghost. And, behold, the veil of the temple was rent in twain from the top to the bottom; and **the earth did quake, and the rocks rent**"* (Matthew 27:50-51). Some believe the rending of the rocks was from the cross to the top of the cave chamber where the Ark of the Covenant was hidden. Jesus' blood flowed down through the cracks in the rock and landed on top of the Ark, onto the Mercy Seat. Matthew 27:52-53 tells how the death of Christ triggered the resurrection of dead saints, *"And the graves were opened; and **many bodies of the saints which slept arose**, And came out of the graves after his resurrection, and went into the holy city, and appeared unto many."* I really don't know how to explain these verses, but it could have been these Scriptures being fulfilled: *"Therefore prophesy and say unto them, Thus saith the Lord God; Behold, O my people, I will open your graves, and cause you to come up out of your graves, and bring you into the land of Israel. And ye shall know that I am the Lord, when I have opened your graves, O my people, and brought you up* *out of your graves"* (Ezekiel 37:12-13). ***"I will ransom them from the power of the grave; I will redeem them from death****: O death, I will be thy plagues; O grave, I will be thy destruction: repentance shall be hid from mine eyes"* (Hosea 13:14).

Look at John 19:34, *"But one of the soldiers with a spear pierced his side, and forthwith came there out blood and water."* They saw that Jesus was dead, so they did not break His legs. The object of piercing the side of Jesus was not to cause death. The piercing of His side caused a deep wound penetrating to His heart. Out flowed blood and water from His side. This signified that Jesus had died from a ruptured heart which caused the surrounding vessels that contained watery fluid to rupture also. He died of a broken heart. Scripture was also fulfilled by Pilate not allowing His legs to be broken. *"He keepeth all his bones: not one of them is broken"* (Psalms 34:20). He was the fulfillment of the Passover lamb described in Exodus 12:46, *"In one house shall it be eaten; thou shalt not carry forth ought of the flesh abroad out of the house;* ***neither shall ye break a bone thereof****."* Perhaps, because blood is produced in the marrow of the bone, this was God's way of telling Satan symbolically that he couldn't touch or stop the blood supply. The water and blood mentioned earlier represents our justification and sanctification.

Read with me the next verse John 19:35, *"And he that saw it bare record, and his record is true: and he knoweth that he saith true, that ye might believe."* Now, consider 1 John 5:5-15, *"Who is he that overcometh the world, but he that believeth that Jesus is the Son of God?* ***This is he that came by water and blood****, even Jesus Christ;* ***not by water only****, but* ***by water and blood****. And it is the Spirit that beareth witness, because the Spirit is truth. For there* are three that bear record in heaven, the Father, the Word, and the Holy Ghost: and these three are one. And there are three that bear witness in earth, the Spirit, and the water, and the blood: and these three agree in one. If we receive the witness of men, the witness of God is greater: for this is the witness of God which he hath testified of his Son. He that believeth on the Son of God hath the witness in himself: he that believeth not God hath made him a liar; because he believeth not the record that God gave of his Son. And this is the record, that God hath given to us eternal life, and this life is in his Son. He that hath the Son hath life; and he that hath not the Son of God hath not life. These things have I written unto you that believe on the name of the Son of God; that ye may know that ye have eternal life, and that ye may believe on the name of the Son of God. And this is the confidence that we have in him, that, if we ask any thing according to his will, he heareth us: And if we know that he hear us, whatsoever we ask, we know that we have the petitions that we desired of him."* The one who bore witness or record was John and his witness was of Jesus.

Next, look at John 4:13-14, *"Jesus answered and said unto her, Whosoever drinketh of this water shall thirst again: But whosoever drinketh of the water that I shall give him shall never thirst; but the water that I shall give him shall be in him a well of water springing up into everlasting life."* Eternal life is the living water. The blood represented Jesus' mortal life or the part that was fully man. Eternal life and the water represents Jesus' spiritual life or the part that was fully God. When Jesus died, His mortal life (blood) and His physical body died. John indicates "eternal life" was manifest in the flesh. We are redeemed through the blood and the manifestation of His Spirit. *"(For the life was manifested, and we have seen it, and bear witness, and shew unto you that eternal life, which was with the Father, and was manifested unto us)"* (1 John 1:2).

4. "My God, my God, why hast thou forsaken me?"

Jesus fourth statement on the cross was only recorded in the Gospels of Matthew and Mark. *"And about the ninth hour Jesus cried with a loud voice, saying, Eli, Eli, lama sabachthani? that is to say,* **My God, my God, why hast thou forsaken me***?"* (Matthew 27:46) *"And at the ninth hour Jesus cried with a loud voice, saying, Eloi, Eloi, lama sabachthani? which is, being interpreted,* **My God, my God, why hast thou forsaken me***?"* (Mark 15:34) After three hours of darkness, Jesus cried out His fourth statement. The ninth hour was three o'clock in the afternoon. Jesus of Nazareth fulfilled the Messianic prophecy of the Suffering Servant in Isaiah 53:12, *"Therefore will I divide him a portion with the great, and he shall divide the spoil with the strong; because he hath poured out his soul unto death: and he was numbered with the transgressors; and he bare the sin of many, and made intercession for the transgressors."* Mark 15:28 reminds us that Jesus fulfilled Isaiah's prophecy, *"And the scripture was fulfilled, which saith, And he was numbered with the transgressors."* Luke 24:46 says something similar, *"And said unto them, Thus it is written, and thus it behooved Christ to suffer, and to rise from the dead the third day."* Jesus spoke these words about the Father forsaking Him as He breathed His last breath. *"And Jesus cried with a loud voice, and gave up the ghost"* (Mark 15:37).

He also fulfilled the words of Psalms 22. King David prophesied of the crucifixion of the Messiah centuries before crucifixion was invented as a method of execution.

Think of the cross as you read Psalms 22:16-18, *"For dogs* [a term used for Gentiles] *have compassed me: the assembly of the wicked have inclosed me: they pierced my hands and my feet. I may tell all my bones: they look and stare upon me. They part my garments among them, and cast lots upon my vesture."*

As if this wasn't enough torture, the burden of all the sins of humanity was put on our Savior. *"Who his own self* **bare our sins in his own body on the tree***, that we, being dead to sins, should live unto righteousness: by whose stripes ye were healed"* (1 Peter 2:24). Jesus cried out in Aramaic in Matthew 27:46, *"Eli, Eli, lama sabachthani? that is to say, My God, my God, why hast thou forsaken me?"* Jesus did not use the word, "Abba, Abba," but the words, "My God, My God." Every time before all His suffering, He called God "Abba, Abba" or "My Father, My Father."

Parallels Between Isaac and Jesus

Notice the parallels with Abraham as he took Isaac up to Mount Moriah, as God the Father led Jesus to Mount Calvary. Isaac carried the wood; Jesus carried the cross. Both Isaac and Jesus were promised sons and were miraculously conceived. Both were called their Father's special "only son." *"And he said, Take now thy son,* **thine only son Isaac***, whom thou lovest, and get thee into the land of Moriah; and offer him there for a burnt offering upon one of the mountains which I will tell thee of"* (Genesis 22:2). *"For God so loved the world, that he gave* **his only begotten Son***, that whosoever believeth in him should not perish, but have everlasting life"* (John 3:16). Both Abraham and God are called "Father." Both Isaac and Jesus were to be a sacrificed to God on the wood. The cross was an altar, *"Forasmuch as ye know that ye were not redeemed with corruptible things, as silver and gold, from your vain conversation received by tradition from your fathers; But with the precious blood of Christ, as of a lamb without blemish and without spot"* (1 Peter 1:18-19). Genesis 22:1, 7-8 tells the story, *"And it came to pass after these things, that God did tempt Abraham, and said unto him, Abraham: and he said, Behold, here I am … And Isaac spake unto Abraham his father, and said, My father: and he said, Here am I, my son. And he said, Behold the fire and the wood: but where is the lamb for a burnt offering? And Abraham said, My son, God will provide himself a lamb for a burnt offering: so they went both of them together."* Both Isaac and Jesus carried their own wood on their back to die on. *"And Abraham **took the wood** of the burnt offering, and **laid it upon Isaac** his son; and he took the fire in his hand, and a knife; and they went both of them together"* (Genesis 22:6). *"Then delivered he him therefore unto them to be crucified. And they took Jesus, and led him away. And he bearing his cross went forth into a place called the place of a skull, which is called in the Hebrew Golgotha"* (John 19:16-17). Both were willing to submit to be sacrificed.

I want you to notice something in Genesis 22:12-14, *"And he said, Lay not thine hand upon the lad, neither do thou any thing unto him: for now I know that thou fearest God, seeing thou hast not withheld thy son, thine only son from me. And Abraham lifted up his eyes, and looked, and behold behind him a ram caught in a thicket by his horns: and Abraham went and took the ram, and offered him up for a burnt offering in the stead of his son. And **Abraham called the name of that place Jehovah-jireh**: as it is said to this day, In the mount of the Lord it shall be* *seen."* The Angel stopped Abraham and turned his focus to a ram caught in the thicket (thorns) by his horns (head). The name of that place is Jehovah-Jireh which means "God will provide" or "The Lord my provider." Both Fathers anticipated their son's resurrection. Genesis 22:5 says, *"And Abraham said unto his young men, Abide ye here with the ass; and I and the lad will go yonder and worship, and* **come again to you***."* Abraham said we will worship and return to you. *"By faith Abraham, when he was tried, offered up Isaac: and he that had received the promises offered up his only begotten son, Of whom it was said, That in Isaac shall thy seed be called:* **Accounting that God was able to raise him up, even from the dead***; from whence also he received him in a figure"* (Hebrews 11: 17-19).

Jesus spoke often of His resurrection. The first two words of His last words on the cross spoken here in Hebrew were "Eli, Eli," (pronounced with a long i sound) means "My God, My God." In the Hebrew Bible, it can be seen that *El, YHWH,* and *Elohim* all refer to the deity of God. The Jewish people would use "Lord" or "Adonai" when reading the Torah or speaking the name of God instead of speaking *EL, YAHWEH,* or *ELOHIM.* And sometimes they would use the word *"Hashem"* meaning "The Name," because they feared mispronouncing the name of God. But Jesus spoke it out on the cross. Can you imagine the look on their faces as Jesus cried out in a loud voice *"Eli, Eli, lama sabach thani"*? *"What shall we then say to these things? If God be for us, who can be against us? He that spared not his own Son, but delivered him up for us all, how shall he not with him also freely give us all things"* (Romans 8:31-32). Jesus had just finished the cup of God's wrath. Nothing had ever come between Jesus and the Father before the sin of the whole world caused the Father to look away. God (El) as Judge of all the earth could not overlook the sins of the world. He could not spare His Son, if He was to save His people and also freely give us all things. God, the righteous Judge, demands justice, but God the Father demands mercy. God as the Father was there, but He had to look away as Jesus absorbed the sin of all humanity.

5. "I thirst."

Let's move on to John 19:28-29 where we find the fifth statement of Christ on the cross, *"After this, Jesus knowing that all things were now accomplished, that the scripture might be fulfilled, saith,* **I thirst.** *Now there was set a vessel full of vinegar: and they filled a sponge with vinegar, and put it upon hyssop, and put it to his mouth."* Have you ever drunk something that tasted so awful that you had to quickly drink something else to remove the taste? He did not receive the vinegar for pain because He didn't want to diminish His suffering for our sake. Isn't it ironic that the One who created every ocean, sea, lake, river, and creek said, "I thirst?" The One who quenched the spiritual thirst of so many others, was physically thirsty at that moment. Even though He knew the sting of vinegar running down into His open wounds would cause Him additional pain, He called for a drink to fulfill the Scriptures. Mark 15:23 adds another detail, *"And they gave him to drink wine mingled with myrrh: but he received it not."* Myrrh, remember, was one of the gifts the wise men brought to baby Jesus. It was used in Bible times for embalming (John 19:39), making perfume (Esther 2:12, Proverbs 7:17), as medicine to reduce swelling, and as an ancient painkiller. So, when Jesus called for a drink, He refused it because He didn't want the myrrh to dull His pain or His awareness as He suffered for us.

6. "It is finished."

With His next breath Jesus spoke His sixth statement from the cross, *"When Jesus therefore had received the vinegar, he said,* **It is finished***: and he bowed his head, and gave up the ghost"* (John 19:30). Mark 15:37 reads, *"And Jesus cried with a loud voice, and gave up the ghost."* When Jesus said, "It is finished," He wasn't just talking about His lifespan or His earthly ministry. Christ's work on the cross, the entire plan of salvation, was complete, done, accomplished, paid in full. Jesus did not say I am finished, but "It is finished." Jesus is still working on your behalf, which we will talk about more later.

The word "finished" used here is actually from the Greek word *tetelestai* which means "paid in full." Jesus has paid the entire penalty, or debt, for our sins. *"Who being the brightness of his glory, and the express image of his person, and upholding all things by the word of his power,* **when he had by himself purged our sins***, sat down on the right hand of the Majesty on high"* (Hebrews 1:3). Hebrews 9:11-12 also speaks of Christ's atoning work, *"But Christ being come an high priest of good things to come, by a greater and more perfect tabernacle, not made with hands, that is to say, not of this building; Neither by the blood of goats and calves, but by his own blood he entered in once into the holy place, having obtained eternal redemption for us."* Also read Hebrews 9:25-28, *"Nor yet that he should offer himself often, as the high priest entereth into the holy place every year with blood of others; For then must he often have suffered since the foundation of the world: but now once in the end of the world hath* *he appeared to put away sin by the sacrifice of himself. And as it is appointed unto men once to die, but after this the judgment: So* **Christ was once offered to bear the sins of many**; *and unto them that look for him shall he appear the second time without sin unto salvation."*

7. "Father, into thy hands I commend my Spirit."

Luke 23:46 adds the seventh and final statement of Jesus on the cross, *"And when Jesus had cried with a loud voice, he said,* **Father, into thy hands I commend my spirit**: *and having said thus, he gave up the ghost."* So, the Father had not left Him, but He had to look away. The Father standing there received His Son's spirit into His hands and the work of redemption was truly finished. While Jesus' physical body was dead and buried, His Spirit returned to the Father until the resurrection.

So, we have studied the physical sufferings and the physical death of Jesus on the cross. This is the central message and the key foundation on which all true Christianity is based. Without Jesus' physical death on the cross, there is no Christianity, there is no eternal salvation for any of us. In this chapter we were trying to make what Jesus went through during this entire, horrific ordeal real to the reader. Once you see exactly what Jesus went through for us, the mental images will be forever etched into your mind. I hope we will never, ever forget the price that Jesus paid to save our souls from eternal damnation and to purchase our redemption.

> *Without Jesus' physical death on the cross, there is no Christianity, there is no eternal salvation for any of us.*

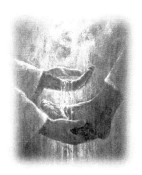

CHAPTER 9

THE RESURRECTION
(John 20)

Before we begin our discussion about the empty tomb, I would like to mention the angels at the tomb. Matthew's and Mark's Gospels relate that one angel spoke to the women, while Luke's and John's Gospel speak of two angels. Mark and Luke called the angels men, probably since angels sometimes appear in the form of men. The angels which appeared to Abraham looked like men, *"And the Lord appeared unto him in the plains of Mamre: and he sat in the tent door in the heat of the day; And he lift up his eyes and looked, and, lo,* **three men stood by him***: and when he saw them, he ran to meet them from the tent door, and bowed himself toward the ground"* (Genesis 18:1-2). Daniel called the angel Gabriel a man, *"Yea, whiles I was speaking in prayer, even* **the man Gabriel***, whom I had seen in the vision at the beginning, being caused to fly swiftly, touched me about the time of the evening oblation"* (Daniel 9:21). Matthew and Mark mentioned only one angel at the tomb, but that one angel spoke to the women. Some say the stories contradict one another. But that is not true. In reading all four accounts, we can see that all four are right by understanding there were two angels. But only one of the two served as the spokesman. With this understanding, there is no reason to consider this a discrepancy in the inerrant Word of God. Plus, remember the four Gospels were written by four different authors with four different perspectives. If you asked four witnesses of an event to describe it, you will get a slightly different version from each one simply because they would emphasize different details based on their perspective. It doesn't mean one is right and the others are wrong. It simply means they recalled different details.

Now, let's dig into John 20, *"The first day of the week cometh Mary Magdalene early, when it was yet dark, unto the sepulchre, and seeth the stone taken away from the sepulchre. Then she runneth, and cometh to Simon Peter, and to the other disciple, whom Jesus loved, and saith unto them, They have taken away the Lord out of the sepulchre, and we know not where they have laid him"* (John 20:1-2). Mary Magdalene came to the tomb of Jesus first and found the stone was taken away and the tomb was empty. At first, she thought someone had stolen His body. In Matthew's account, it says when the two women went to the tomb, there was an earthquake. In Mark, it says that when the three women went to the tomb, they saw the stone rolled away. You can explain it like this, as they were approaching the tomb of Jesus, an earthquake occurred at that very moment and the stone rolled away at their arrival. Let me continue to put this all together for you, regarding the number of the women coming to the tomb. I believe at least five women came to the tomb. Luke named three (Mary Magdalene, Joanna, and Mary the mother of James—Luke 24:10) and then says "other women" went too. Matthew does not say that only two women were there, but he only mentioned Mary Magdalene and the "other Mary" (Matthew 28:1).

Mark does not say only three were there, but he mentioned Mary Magdalene, Mary the mother of James, and Salome (Mark 16:1). They only focused on the women they named. John only named Mary Magdalene, but look at John 20:2 closely, *"Then she runneth, and cometh to Simon Peter, and to the other disciple, whom Jesus loved, and saith unto them, They have taken away the Lord out of the sepulchre, and we know not where they have laid him."* When she said, "**we** know not where they have laid him," it is clear that she was not alone.

Let's continue reading John 20:3-4, *"Peter therefore went forth, and that other disciple, and came to the sepulchre. So they ran both together: and the other disciple did outrun Peter, and came first to the sepulchre."* Peter and John ran together toward the tomb, but John outran Peter and came to the tomb first. They ran to see for themselves if what Mary said was true. *"And he stooping down, and looking in, saw the linen clothes lying; yet went he not in. Then cometh Simon Peter following him, and went into the sepulchre, and seeth the linen clothes lie, And the napkin, that was about his head, not lying with the linen clothes, but wrapped together in a place by itself. Then went in also that other disciple, which came first to the sepulchre, and he saw, and believed. For as yet they knew not the scripture, that he must rise again from the dead. Then the disciples went away again unto their own home"* (John 20:5-10). Verse 5 says, *"John stooping down and looking in"* (the Greek word used for "looking in" is *blepo* means "to clearly see a material"). He clearly saw the grave clothes and the napkin. When they entered, they did not see the body of Jesus, but they saw the grave clothes in a certain order. Why did John write the head napkin was "wrapped together in a place by itself"? John

20:8-9 above, tells us when John saw the arrangement of the grave clothes, he believed. I am convinced, as many others are, that the grave clothes were lying exactly as the body of Jesus had laid in them. Still wrapped, no one had to loose Jesus or remove the cloths. He just came out of the grave clothes or passed right through them. Linen clothes referred to the manner in which they prepared the body for burial in that day. They would wrap the linen around the entire body until they reached the neck. John saw the linen clothes laying just as they had been when the body of Jesus laid within them, but now there was no body. The wrapped, linen clothes were empty.

THE EMBALMING OF JESUS' BODY

We read about the preparation of His body by Nicodemus and Joseph of Arimathea in John 19:39-40, *"And there came also Nicodemus, which at the first came to Jesus by night, and brought a mixture of myrrh and aloes, about an hundred pound weight. Then took they the body of Jesus, and wound it in linen clothes with the spices, as the manner of the Jews is to bury."* As they wrapped the linen clothes around the body of Jesus, they poured 100 pounds of spices into the wrappings and upon the body of Jesus. All these liquid spices would settle and harden around the body of Jesus. These spices were used to combat the smell of a decomposing corpse. When Peter and John saw the empty linens, they knew it was inconceivable to think that someone had stolen His body out of the grave clothes bound together around Him. They would have stuck to His body and would have been very difficult to remove intact. The two disciples saw the linen clothes lying uncut, undisturbed, just as they had been, but there is no body inside. They had to believe that

THE RESURRECTION (John 20)

the body of Jesus was miraculously removed. Look back at John 20:7, *"And the napkin, that was about his head, not lying with the linen clothes, but wrapped together in a place by itself."* The Greek word translated "wrapped together" actually means "twisted together."

In John 20:11-12 *"But Mary stood without at the sepulchre weeping: and as she wept, she stooped down, and looked into the sepulchre, And seeth two angels in white sitting, the one at the head, and the other at the feet, where the body of Jesus had lain."* Peter and John left Mary at the tomb weeping and when she looked in, she saw two angels, one at the head, and one at the feet of where Jesus had laid. If we just read over it too quickly, we will miss something significant. I believe she saw a spiritual replica of the Ark of the Covenant and the mercy seat. Remember, the Ark of the Covenant had two cherubim (angels) on top of it, one on either side. *"For if the blood of bulls and of goats, and the ashes of an heifer sprinkling the unclean, sanctifieth to the purifying of the flesh: How much more shall the blood of Christ, who through the eternal Spirit offered himself without spot to God, purge your conscience from dead works to serve the living God?"* (Hebrews 9:13-14). Romans 3:25 speaks of Christ's atoning work, *"Whom God hath set forth to be a **propitiation** through faith in his blood, to declare his righteousness for the remission of sins that are past, through the forbearance of God."* In 1 John 2:2, 10, John echoes Paul's words, *"And he is the **propitiation** for our sins: and not for ours only, but also for the sins of the whole world*

> I believe she saw a spiritual replica of the Ark of the Covenant and the mercy seat.

*... Herein is love, not that we loved God, but that he loved us, and sent his Son to be the **propitiation** for our sins."* The word "propitiation" is from the Greek word *hilasterion*, and specifically means the "Mercy Seat." In other words, Jesus is our atoning sacrifice and our blood-sprinkled Mercy Seat. The High Priest sprinkled blood on the Mercy Seat seven times on the Day of Atonement annually (Leviticus 16:14). So, God saw His people through the blood instead of through the broken law.

In Exodus 25:17-22, God gave Moses instructions for the golden lid of the Ark of the Covenant, *"And thou shalt make a mercy seat of pure gold: two cubits and a half shall be the length thereof, and a cubit and a half the breadth thereof. And thou shalt make two cherubims of gold, of beaten work shalt thou make them, in the two ends of the mercy seat. And make one cherub on the one end, and the other cherub on the other end: even of the mercy seat shall ye make the cherubims on the two ends thereof. And the cherubims shall stretch forth their wings on high, covering the mercy seat with their wings, and their faces shall look one to another; toward the mercy seat shall the faces of the cherubims be. And thou shalt put **the mercy seat above upon the ark**; and in the ark thou shalt put the testimony that I shall give thee. And there I will meet with thee, and I will commune with thee from above the mercy seat, from between the two cherubims which are upon the ark of the testimony, of all things which I will give thee in commandment unto the children of Israel."*

Hebrews 9:4-5 also describes the Ark, *"The ark of the covenant overlaid round about with gold, wherein was the golden pot that had manna, and Aaron's rod that budded, and the tables of the covenant; and over it the cherubims of glory shadowing the mercy seat; of which we cannot now speak particularly."* Most people don't realize the Hebrew word translated "Ark" means "coffin or chest" and the linen clothes wound around a buried body was called a "casket." The Mercy Seat, when Jesus was raised, became a throne of grace.

CHRIST—OUR HEAVENLY HIGH PRIEST

Hebrews 9:11-15 describes how Christ interceded and intervened for us as our heavenly High Priest, *"But Christ being come an high priest of good things to come, by a greater and more perfect tabernacle, not made with hands, that is to say, not of this building; Neither by the blood of goats and calves, but by his own blood he entered in once into the holy place, having obtained eternal redemption for us. For if the blood of bulls and of goats, and the ashes of an heifer sprinkling the unclean, sanctifieth to the purifying of the flesh: How much more shall the blood of Christ, who through the eternal Spirit offered himself without spot to God, purge your conscience from dead works to serve the living God? And for this cause he is the mediator of the new testament, that by means of death, for the redemption of the transgressions that were under the first testament, they which are called might receive the promise of eternal inheritance."*

The blood of Jesus being applied, changes the throne of judgment into a throne of grace. *"Seeing then that we have a great high priest, that is passed into the heavens, Jesus the Son of God, let us hold fast our profession. For we have not an high priest which cannot be touched with the feeling of our infirmities; but was in all points tempted like as we are, yet without sin. Let us therefore come boldly unto the throne of grace, that we may obtain mercy, and find grace to help in time of need"* (Hebrews 4:14-16). By the application of the blood of Jesus, the Mercy Seat becomes a place we can come to boldly and find supernatural help because it has become a place of spiritual communion. The Ark of the Covenant was a sign of God's covenant with Israel. What Mary saw symbolically in the empty tomb was the New Covenant and Jesus as the Mercy Seat.

What Mary saw symbolically in the empty tomb was the New Covenant and Jesus as the Mercy Seat.

John 20:13-17 records Mary's encounter with her risen Savior, *"And they say unto her, Woman, why weepest thou? She saith unto them, Because they have taken away my Lord, and I know not where they have laid him. And when she had thus said, she turned herself back, and saw Jesus standing, and knew not that it was Jesus. Jesus saith unto her, Woman, why weepest thou? whom seekest thou? She, supposing him to be the gardener, saith unto him, Sir, if thou have borne him hence, tell me where thou hast laid him, and I will take him away. Jesus saith unto her, Mary. She turned herself, and saith unto him, Rabboni; which is to say, Master. Jesus saith unto her, Touch me not; for I am not yet ascended to my Father: but go to my brethren, and say unto them, I ascend unto my Father, and your Father; and to my God, and your God."*

Even after seeing the angel, Mary still didn't understand what he had told her and thought someone had stolen Jesus' body. One writer made the assertion that the stone had been rolled away from the grave, but not from her heart. In verse 14, she saw Jesus, but didn't realize it was Him. Look at John 20:15 above, she supposed Jesus to be the gardener or the caretaker of the cemetery. But when

Jesus spoke her name, "Mary," she knew Him. She turned and said to Him, "Rabboni" which means "Master." She tried to embrace Him, but He instructed her, "No, go tell my brethren."

Jesus didn't look like the Jesus she knew, but she recognized His voice. Jesus said, "Touch me not." The Greek word translated "touch" here means "to attach oneself to, to fasten to." Other versions render that phrase "stop clinging to me" or "do not hold on to me." Mary wanted to cling to Jesus. Do you blame her? She had just witnessed her Savior tortured, crucified, and buried but now He was ALIVE. No wonder she wanted to cling to Him, but He wanted her to go tell His brethren that He was risen from the dead. Jesus said, *"I ascend unto my Father and your Father, and to My God and your God."* Jesus was saying there is a difference now because He was going back to the Father. You are not coming to God as your Judge, but as "Abba, Daddy" through His blood. They went from disciples to brethren.

Wow! What a promotion bought with the resurrection! This phrase "My brethren" speaks to the love Jesus had for them and His confidence in them to fulfill the mission He was about to give them. Jesus told us what this title, "My brethren," meant earlier in His ministry, *"Then one said unto him, Behold, thy mother and thy brethren stand without, desiring to speak with thee. But he answered and said unto him that told him, Who is my mother? and **who are my brethren**? And he stretched forth his hand toward his disciples, and said, Behold my mother and my brethren! **For whosoever shall do the will of my Father which is in heaven, the same is my brother, and sister, and mother**"* (Matthew 12:47-50). Paul also alluded to this in Romans 8:29, *"For whom he did foreknow, he also did* *predestinate to be conformed to the image of his Son, that he might be* **the firstborn among many brethren.**"

Now let's look at John 20:19-23, *"Then the same day at evening, being the first day of the week, when the doors were shut where the disciples were assembled for fear of the Jews, came Jesus and stood in the midst, and saith unto them, Peace be unto you. And when he had so said, he shewed unto them his hands and his side. Then were the disciples glad, when they saw the Lord. Then said Jesus to them again, Peace be unto you: as my Father hath sent me, even so send I you. And when he had said this, he breathed on them, and saith unto them, Receive ye the Holy Ghost: Whose soever sins ye remit, they are remitted unto them; and whose soever sins ye retain, they are retained."*

The disciples had a face-to-face encounter with the resurrected Jesus. Because of their fear of the Jews, they had locked the doors. But Jesus appeared and stood in their midst. After they had forsaken Jesus at the cross, and Peter denied Him, the disciples probably feared Jesus would rebuke them. John might have thought Jesus would ask, "Why aren't you watching after my mother." They most likely were expecting some words of rebuke. Instead, He spoke a word of reconciliation to them, "Peace be unto you."

Look at 2 Corinthians 5:18-20, *"And all things are of God, who hath* **reconciled** *us to himself by Jesus Christ, and hath given to us the ministry of reconciliation; To wit, that God was in Christ,* **reconciling the world unto himself***, not imputing their trespasses unto them; and hath committed unto us* **the word of reconciliation***. Now then we are ambassadors for Christ, as though God did beseech* *you by us: we pray you in Christ's stead,* **be ye reconciled to God**.*"* Jesus was preparing them for this ministry of reconciliation. *"For it pleased the Father that in him should all fulness dwell; And, having made peace through the blood of his cross, by him* **to reconcile all things unto himself***; by him, I say, whether they be things in earth, or things in heaven"* (Colossians 1:19-20).

The blood of Jesus was shed to reconcile us or to restore our broken relationship with God. It was to bring mankind back into peace and harmony with God. Adam brought death, but Jesus brought peace and life. Notice the last words of 2 Corinthians 5:20, *"Now then we are ambassadors for Christ, as though God did beseech you by us: we pray you in Christ's stead,* **be ye reconciled to God***."* "Be ye reconciled to God." Because of the death of Jesus, God is not counting our sins against us, if we will just make the choice to accept the gift of grace no matter how bad our sin is. However, we do have a part to play. We must be reconciled to God!

Ten of the disciples were present in the room where Jesus appeared, all except Thomas. It was good that the disciples had stayed together. Jesus' resurrected body wasn't limited by locked doors, He miraculously stood in their midst. He could appear or vanish at will. Luke's Gospel mentions this gathering and includes others with them—*"And they rose up the same hour, and returned to Jerusalem, and found the eleven gathered together, and them that were with them"* (Luke 24:33). Jesus invited them also to actually touch His body to see that it was real. *"Behold my hands and my feet, that it is I myself: handle me, and see; for a spirit hath not flesh and bones, as ye see me have. And when he had thus spoken, he shewed them his hands and his feet"* (Luke 24:39-40). Then

Jesus ate some fish and a piece of a honeycomb to prove to them He was real and not just a spirit (Luke 24:41).

A FORETASTE OF PENTECOST

"And when he had said this, he breathed on them, and saith unto them, Receive ye the Holy Ghost" (John 20:22). This very event happened on the day of Firstfruits. Does this mean they received the Holy Spirit at that time? I believe it was only a foretaste and a promise of what the disciples would soon receive at Pentecost. It was a type of firstfruits of the coming harvest during the Feast of Weeks or Pentecost. Jesus had said earlier, *"He that believeth on me, as the scripture hath said, out of his belly shall flow rivers of living water. (But this spake he of the Spirit, which they that believe on him should receive:* **for the Holy Ghost was not yet given**; *because that Jesus was not yet glorified.)"* (John 7:38-39). The promise was that they would receive the Holy Spirit after He ascended into heaven and became glorified. Jesus told His disciples to tarry at Jerusalem until they were endued with power from on high.

"And said unto them, Thus it is written, and thus it behoved Christ to suffer, and to rise from the dead the third day: And that repentance and remission of sins should be preached in his name among all nations, beginning at Jerusalem. And ye are witnesses of these things. And, behold, I send the promise of my Father upon you: but **tarry ye in the city of Jerusalem, until ye be endued with power from on high**" (Luke 24:46-49). Jesus also instructed them to wait for the infilling of the Spirit in Acts 1:4-5, 8, *"And, being assembled together with them, commanded them that they should not depart from Jerusalem, but* **wait for the promise of the Father**,

which, saith he, ye have heard of me. For John truly baptized with water; but **ye shall be baptized with the Holy Ghost not many days hence** *... But ye shall receive power, after that the Holy Ghost is come upon you: and ye shall be witnesses unto me both in Jerusalem, and in all Judaea, and in Samaria, and unto the uttermost part of the earth."* The act of breathing on them was a promise of what was coming. Pentecost was the fulfillment of that promise in Luke 24:49, *"And, behold, I send the promise of my Father upon you: but tarry ye in the city of Jerusalem, until ye be endued with power from on high."* The word "until" above and the phrase "ye shall receive," both indicate it hadn't happened yet. In Acts 2:32-33, Peter explained what happened on Pentecost, *"This Jesus hath God raised up, whereof we all are witnesses. Therefore being by the right hand of God exalted, and* **having received of the Father the promise of the Holy Ghost***, he hath shed forth this, which ye now see and hear."*

Jesus was the firstfruits of Passover. However, the Day of Pentecost was the fruit of Jesus' death, burial, resurrection, ascension, and glorification just as Jesus had promised. What the disciples received when Jesus breathed on them was a foretaste of the baptism of the Holy Spirit. Jesus breathing upon His disciples symbolized the Spirit of God. In fact, the Greek word pneuma is translated "life, breath, spirit, and wind" in the New Testament. So, the Holy Spirit is the life and breath of God. Remember, man was made a living soul by the breath of God in the beginning of creation. *"And the Lord God formed man of the dust of the ground, and* **breathed into his nostrils the breath of life; and man became a living soul**" (Genesis 2:7). Jesus likened being born of the Spirit to wind or breath.

Jesus said to Nicodemus in John 3:8, *"The wind bloweth where it listeth, and thou hearest the sound thereof, but canst not tell whence it cometh, and whither it goeth: so is every one that is born of the Spirit."*

Ezekiel prophesied of the dead, dry bones being revived and restored to life by the breath of God, *"Then said he unto me, Prophesy unto the wind, prophesy, son of man, and say to the wind, Thus saith the Lord God; Come from the four winds, O breath, and breathe upon these slain, that they may live. So I prophesied as he commanded me, and the breath came into them, and they lived, and stood up upon their feet, an exceeding great army. Then he said unto me, Son of man, these bones are the whole house of Israel: behold, they say, Our bones are dried, and our hope is lost: we are cut off for our parts. Therefore prophesy and say unto them, Thus saith the Lord God; Behold, O my people, I will open your graves, and cause you to come up out of your graves, and bring you into the land of Israel. And ye shall know that I am the Lord, when I have opened your graves, O my people, and brought you up out of your graves, And shall put my spirit in you, and ye shall live, and I shall place you in your own land: then shall ye know that I the Lord have spoken it, and performed it, saith the Lord"* (Ezekiel 37:9-14).

Notice when the Holy Spirit came into the upper room that He sounded like a rushing mighty wind, *"And suddenly there came a sound from heaven **as of a rushing mighty wind**, and it filled all the house where they were sitting"* (Acts 2:2). This description makes me think of the blowing of the Shofar or ram's horn. The Shofar makes no sound without breath blowing through it. This also happened at Mount Sinai at the first Pentecost or the giving of the law, *"And when the voice of the trumpet sounded* *long, and waxed louder and louder, Moses spake, and God answered him by a voice"* (Exodus 19:19). Hebrews 12:19 refers to when Moses went to the mountain and a great fear came on the people as they heard God's voice, *"And **the sound of a trumpet, and the voice of words**; which voice they that heard intreated that the word should not be spoken to them any more."* This wind was felt and heard. Even as the wind, the breath, and the Spirit of God had moved upon the face of the waters before God spoke "Let there be Light." God quickened everything into life and existence with His breathed Word. *"And the earth was without form, and void; and darkness was upon the face of the deep. And t**he Spirit of God moved upon the face of the waters**. And God said, Let there be light: and there was light"* (Genesis 1:2-3).

THE BREATH OF GOD

The most wonderful example of God's breath is found in Acts 2:2-4, *"And suddenly there came a sound from heaven as of a rushing mighty wind, and it filled all the house where they were sitting. And there appeared unto them cloven tongues like as of fire, and it sat upon each of them. And they were all filled with the Holy Ghost, and began to speak with other tongues, as the Spirit gave them utterance."* This was the fulfillment of the disciple's foretaste in John 20:22—*"And when he had said this, **he breathed on them**, and saith unto them, **Receive ye the Holy Ghost**."* The promise become a reality on the Day of Pentecost. Look at Acts 2:39, *"For the promise is unto you, and to your children, and to all that are afar off, even as many as the Lord our God shall call."* Peter told those Jews that it was unto you (the Jews of that day), and your children (the whole nation of Israel), and to all that are afar off (Gentiles), as many as the Lord our God shall call. God was simply saying, the reality of the promise is for everyone. Jesus performed this act upon ten of the eleven disciples. Thomas was not present for whatever reason. Jesus breathed *on* them, but on Pentecost, He breathed *in* them. The outpouring of the Holy Spirit was on the Day of Pentecost being fulfilled which was also known as the Feast of Harvest. It could not happen before that day, just as Jesus could not have died on the cross a day sooner than Passover. So, in John 20, Jesus was not imparting the Holy Spirit to them. He was promising to do so later at Pentecost.

John tells us that Jesus showed the disciples His scars, not once, but twice. Jesus came through the locked door and appeared before the disciples who were extremely frightened. Jesus made it a point to show His scars to them. The other disciples told Thomas, but he didn't believe at first. *"The other disciples therefore said unto him, We have seen the Lord. But he said unto them, Except I shall see in his hands the print of the nails, and put my finger into the print of the nails, and thrust my hand into his side, I will not believe"* (John 20:25). Eight days later, Jesus visited the disciples again and this time, Thomas was present. *"Then saith he to Thomas, Reach hither thy finger, and behold my hands; and reach hither thy hand, and thrust it into my side: and be not faithless, but believing. And Thomas answered and said unto him, My Lord and my God. Jesus saith unto him, Thomas, because thou hast seen me, thou hast believed: blessed are they that have not seen, and yet have believed"* (John 20:27-29).

You may ask, "Why did Jesus show His wounds to His disciples after His resurrection?" Look at Acts 1:3, *"To whom also he shewed himself alive after his passion* **by**

many infallible proofs, *being seen of them forty days, and speaking of the things pertaining to the kingdom of God."* It was an infallible proof that He was the same person. Jesus said, "Behold My hands and reach hither thy hand, and thrust it into My side." He was identifying Himself as the same Jesus they had followed but in a resurrected body. They had never seen Him this way before. Peter, James, and John had seen Him transfigured, His garments white as snow, but never like this. So, they were tempted to doubt Him. But when they saw the nail prints in His hands and His pierced side, they believed. These marks they could not dispute. It was infallible proof. The Greek word translated as the phrase "infallible proofs" is *tekmeriois*. It refers to that which causes something or someone to be known in a convincing and decisive manner. Jesus spent time with them, He walked and talked, and even ate with them after the resurrection. These are some amazing facts that are infallible proofs.

THE RESURRECTED REDEEMER REVEALED

The women worshipped Him and held His nailed-scarred feet. *"And as they went to tell his disciples, behold, Jesus met them, saying, All hail. And they came and **held him by the feet**, and worshipped him"* (Matthew 28:9). Jesus broke bread with Cleopas and another unnamed disciple. Then, after He had convinced them with the Scriptures, their eyes were opened, *"And it came to pass, as he sat at meat with them, he took bread, and blessed it, and brake, and gave to them. **And their eyes were opened, and they knew him; and he vanished out of their sight**. And they said one to another, Did not our heart burn within us, while he talked with us by the way, and while he opened to us the scriptures? And they rose up* *the same hour, and returned to Jerusalem, and found the eleven gathered together, and them that were with them, Saying, The Lord is risen indeed, and hath appeared to Simon"* (Luke 24:30-34).

Fred, Hannah, and Connie at the garden tomb in Jerusalem.

When their eyes were opened, and they knew it was Jesus, and He vanished out of their sight. They immediately ran and told the eleven disciples what happened. *"And they told what things were done in the way, and how he was known of them in breaking of bread. And as they thus spake, Jesus himself stood in the midst of them, and saith unto them, Peace be unto you"* (Luke 24:35-36). As they were telling the disciples what happened, Jesus suddenly appeared before them. Luke 24:37-40 records their reaction, *"But they were terrified and affrighted, and supposed that they had seen a spirit. And he said unto them, Why are ye troubled? and why do thoughts arise in your hearts? Behold my hands and my feet, that it is I myself: handle me, and see; for a spirit hath not flesh and bones, as ye see me have. And when he had thus spoken, he shewed them his hands and his feet."* The rest of the story is recorded in John 21. Jesus showed His scars as proof, and then ate fish and a honeycomb with them. Some still didn't believe. *"And **while they yet believed not for joy,** and wondered, he said unto them, Have ye here any meat? And they gave him a piece of a broiled fish, and of an honeycomb. And he took it, and did eat before them"* (Luke 24:41-43).

Then, in Luke 24:44-49, Jesus explained how His death, burial, and resurrection fulfilled the Scriptures, *"And he said unto them, These are the words which I spake unto you, while I was yet with you, that all things must be fulfilled, which were written in the law of Moses, and in the prophets, and in the psalms, concerning me. Then opened he their understanding, that they might understand the scriptures, And said unto them, Thus it is written, and thus it behooved Christ to suffer, and to rise from the dead the third day: And that repentance and remission of sins should be preached in his name among all nations, beginning at Jerusalem. And ye are witnesses of these things. And, behold, I send the promise of my Father upon you: but tarry ye in the city of Jerusalem, until ye be endued with power from on high."*

When He spoke this time, He opened their understanding of the Scriptures. Finally, read with me John 20:30-31, *"And many other signs truly did Jesus in the presence of his disciples, which are not written in this book: But these are written, that ye might believe that Jesus is the Christ, the Son of God; and that believing ye might have life through his name."* This is John's reason for writing his Gospel—so we might believe that Jesus is the Christ, the Anointed One, the Messiah, and the only begotten Son of God. The only way to enter eternal life is through the power of His name. In John 20, Jesus went to great lengths to equip His followers with faith and understanding of the Scriptures concerning His resurrection. Their sorrow was turned into joy. This is a

> *"Believe that Jesus is the Christ, the Son of God; and that believing ye might have life through his name."*

great picture of what happens when we enter into eternal life by the only, true, and living way—JESUS CHRIST!

CHAPTER 10

THE RESTORATION OF PETER
(John 21)

John 21 is the story of the restoration and commission of both Peter and everyone who chooses to give their lives to serve in God's kingdom. Let's set the stage by reading John 21:1-3, *"After these things Jesus shewed himself again to the disciples at the sea of Tiberias; and on this wise shewed he himself. There were together Simon Peter, and Thomas called Didymus, and Nathanael of Cana in Galilee, and the sons of Zebedee, and two other of his disciples. Simon Peter saith unto them,* **I go a fishing**. *They say unto him, We also go with thee. They went forth, and entered into a ship immediately; and that night they caught nothing."* At this point Peter decided to quit the ministry and to go back to his old career, what he did before he ever met Jesus—fishing! Remember, he denied Jesus three times and he probably felt unworthy to ever be used of God again. Notice the influence Peter had which explains why Satan fought him so hard. When Peter went fishing, the other disciples followed him. The fact that they caught nothing reminds me of John 15:5, *"Without me you can do nothing."*

Now, let's read the next part in John 21:4-14, *"But when the morning was now come, Jesus stood on the shore: but the disciples knew not that it was Jesus. Then Jesus saith unto them, Children, have ye any meat? They answered him, No. And he said unto them, Cast the net on the right side of the ship, and ye shall find. They cast therefore, and now they were not able to draw it for the multitude of fishes. Therefore that disciple whom Jesus loved saith unto Peter, It is the Lord. Now when Simon Peter heard that it was the Lord, he girt his fisher's coat unto him, (for he was naked,) and did cast himself into the sea. And the other disciples came in a little ship; (for they were not far from land, but as it were two hundred cubits,) dragging the net with fishes. As soon then as they were come to land, they saw a fire of coals there, and fish laid thereon, and bread. Jesus saith unto them, Bring of the fish which ye have now caught. Simon Peter went up, and drew the net to land full of great fishes, an hundred and fifty and three: and for all there were so many, yet was not the net broken. Jesus saith unto them, Come and dine. And none of the disciples durst ask him, Who art thou? knowing that it was the Lord. Jesus then cometh, and taketh bread, and giveth them, and fish likewise. This is now the third time that Jesus shewed himself to his disciples, after that he was risen from the dead."*

This was a miraculous catch of fish. Fisherman usually fished at night and would sell the fish in the morning at the marketplace. They had fished all night long without catching even one fish. They were on the Sea of Tiberias, better known as the Sea of Galilee. Verse 2 tells us seven disciples went fishing—Simon Peter, Thomas called Didymus, Nathaniel, the sons of Zebedee (James and John), and two other unnamed disciples. Thomas was called "Didymus" which means "twin." There is no indication in the Bible who his twin might have been. There are several traditions, but I don't find any proof that has convinced me of who Thomas' twin was. John, the writer, obviously knew but doesn't reveal it to us.

Peter decided to go back to fishing. Peter, James, and John were some of the first disciples of Jesus. Peter's initial encounter with Jesus in Luke 5:1-11, which occurred over three years earlier, was remarkably similar to the account we just read in John 21, *"And it came to pass, that, as the people pressed upon him to hear the word of God, he stood by the lake of Gennesaret, And saw two ships standing by the lake: but the fishermen were gone out of them, and were washing their nets. And he entered into one of the ships, which was Simon's, and prayed him that he would thrust out a little from the land. And he sat down, and taught the people out of the ship. Now when he had left speaking, he said unto Simon, Launch out into the deep, and let down your nets for a draught. And Simon answering said unto him, Master, we have toiled all the night, and have taken nothing: nevertheless at thy word I will let down the net. And when they had this done, they inclosed a great multitude of fishes: and their net brake. And they beckoned unto their partners, which were in the other ship, that they should come and help them. And they came, and filled both the ships, so that they began to sink. When Simon Peter saw it, he fell down at Jesus' knees, saying, Depart from me; for I am a sinful man, O Lord. For he was astonished, and all that were with him, at the draught of the fishes which they had taken: And so was also James, and John, the sons of Zebedee, which were partners with Simon. And Jesus said unto Simon, Fear not; from henceforth thou shalt catch men. And when they had brought their ships to land, they forsook all, and followed him."*

I can't say for sure, but I believe these two encounters with Christ happened at the same place on the Sea of Galilee. In the three years they traveled with Jesus, Peter, James, and John had witnessed amazing things as His disciples. They had witnessed His mighty miracles, healings, and deliverances. They saw Him after the resurrection, but still returned to their old ways. Do not judge them too harshly, we all would have probably done the same thing—fished for fish instead of fishing for men. Peter persuaded the others to go back with him, but they did not do very well fishing.

THE SIGNIFICANCE OF 153 FISH

That morning Jesus stood on the shore but, at first, they did not recognize Him. He told them to cast their empty nets on the other side of the boat. They got such a miraculous catch they were unable to draw it in. John, recognizing Jesus, immediately told Peter, "It is the Lord." Peter was fishing without his outer garment on, so he put his fisher's coat on (the coat he had forsaken before to follow Jesus). Luke 5:11 says, *"And when they had brought their ships to land, they forsook all, and followed him."* Here in John 21:7, when Peter realized it was Jesus, he jumped out of the boat and started swimming to shore. *"And the other disciples came in a little ship; (for they were not far from land, but as it were two hundred cubits [or about 100 yards],) dragging the net with fishes"* (John 21:8). The other disciples brought the fish to the shore. *"As soon then as they were come to land, they saw a fire of coals there, and fish laid thereon, and bread. Jesus saith unto them, Bring of the fish which ye have now caught"* (John 21:9-10). Remember, all except John had forsaken Jesus. Can you imagine Peter's thoughts? Something like,

THE RESTORATION OF PETER (John 21)

"I denied him three times even after I swore that I would lay down my life for Jesus." Peter probably replayed the scene from John 13:37-38 in his mind, *"Peter said unto him, Lord, why cannot I follow thee now? I will lay down my life for thy sake. Jesus answered him, Wilt thou lay down thy life for my sake? Verily, verily, I say unto thee, The cock shall not crow, till thou hast denied me thrice."* Peter was well aware of his failings and shortcomings. We all must admit we have them too. Peter had reverted back to his old life of fishing for fish. When Peter swam to the shore, Jesus had no words of condemnation for Peter, but said, *"Bring of the fish which ye have now caught"* to me.

What was the significance of 153 fish?

What was the significance of 153 fish? Some scholars suggest that the Jews at that time believed there were 153 species of fish found in the Sea of Galilee and 153 nations in the world then. Jesus may have been using a tradition Peter and these other fishermen were familiar with to send a message to them to share the Gospel with everyone as fishers of men. I also discovered in my study something interesting I had never heard or read before. Scripture speaks of Jesus personally blessing people 153 times. The book of Mark records that Jesus Christ on 3 occasions individually blessed 3 people. The book of Matthew records on 23 occasions where Jesus blessed a total of 47 people. The book of Luke records on 14 occasions where Jesus blessed 94 people. The book of John records 8 occasions where Jesus blessed a total of 9 people. All together, Jesus directly blessed 153 people in 48 separate incidents. In this is Jesus telling us how to be blessed and bless others?

Jesus was also teaching here, I will let you catch men,

but bring them to me. *"Simon Peter went up, and drew the net to land full of great fishes, an hundred and fifty and three: and for all there were so many, yet was not the net broken. Jesus saith unto them, Come and dine. And none of the disciples durst ask him, Who art thou? knowing that it was the Lord"* (John 21:11-12). Notice in the first story in Luke, their nets broke. *"And when they had this done, they inclosed a great multitude of fishes: **and their net brake**"* (Luke 5:6). But in John 21:11 above, their nets were not broken. It is clearly stated in the first incident, that the net broke and in the second incident, the net did not break. In Luke 5, they were still fishers of fish. But Jesus was saying in John 21, you are no longer fishers of fish, but fishers of men. In Luke 5, they drew the fish in their own strength, and they lost some, but the disciples here in John 21, drew in the fish with the Lord's help. The Lord was saying, "I won't just get them in the net for you, I will help you also to bring them all the way to me."

In John 21:12, Jesus invited the disciples to "come and dine," or come have breakfast with me. Jesus often used meals to fellowship with people and used that time to teach them spiritual truths. In the book of Luke alone, there are ten stories of Jesus dining with people. With the two disciples He met on the road to Emmaus, Jesus expounded the Word of God over food. At this point in the story, all the disciples were there with Jesus to eat breakfast. *"And the other disciples came in a little ship; (for they were not far from land, but as it were two hundred cubits,) dragging the net with fishes"* (John 21:8). This verse lets us know that the other disciples were there also. It was a family breakfast with Jesus. *"Jesus then cometh, and taketh bread, and giveth them, and fish likewise. This is now the third time that Jesus shewed himself to his disciples, after that he was risen from the dead"* (John 21:13-14).

Now let's read John 21:15-17 where Jesus reissued Peter's call to the ministry: *"So when they had dined, Jesus saith to Simon Peter, Simon, son of Jonas, lovest thou me more than these? He saith unto him, Yea, Lord; thou knowest that I love thee. He saith unto him, Feed my lambs. He saith to him again the second time, Simon, son of Jonas, lovest thou me? He saith unto him, Yea, Lord; thou knowest that I love thee. He saith unto him, Feed my sheep. He saith unto him the third time, Simon, son of Jonas, lovest thou me? Peter was grieved because he said unto him the third time, Lovest thou me? And he said unto him, Lord, thou knowest all things; thou knowest that I love thee. Jesus saith unto him, Feed my sheep."* This exchange between Peter and the risen Lord represents Peter being restored back to his ministry. Jesus did this publicly in front of all the other disciples.

I believe Peter was struggling with his denial of Jesus. In Mark 16:7, the angel told the women who came to the empty tomb, *"But go your way, tell his disciples **and Peter** that he goeth before you into Galilee: there shall ye see him, as he said unto you."* "Go … tell his disciples and PETER …" When Peter heard those words, they must have rung in his ears. Peter probably questioned to himself, "Did the angel really call me by name?" The angel said this to show Peter that Jesus had not rejected him as the commissioned leader because of his failure. That very day, Jesus met Peter alone to reassure him and restore him. *"The Lord is risen indeed, and **hath appeared to Simon**"* (Luke 24:34). 1 Corinthians 15:5 indicates that *"he was **seen of Cephas**, then of the twelve."* Cephas is a nickname Jesus gave to Peter which means "a rock" or "a stone" (John 1:42). Jesus knew from the moment He met

Peter that his rock-solid faith would later become part of the foundation of the New Testament Church. This conversation in John 21 took place in front of all the disciples. Jesus also started up the conversation with Peter. Remember, Peter had denied Jesus three times, so Jesus required a three-fold confirmation of Peter's love and loyalty to Him. When we fall and return back to Jesus, He doesn't just heal you personally, but will restore you publicly, as is seen in the story of the prodigal.

Look with me at Jesus' first question to Peter, *"So when they had dined, Jesus saith to Simon Peter, Simon, son of Jonas,* **lovest thou me more than these***? He saith unto him, Yea, Lord; thou knowest that I love thee. He saith unto him, Feed my lambs"* (John 21:15). Jesus, speaking to Peter this time, didn't call him Peter, but Simon, son of Jonas (or Jonah). Jesus said it publicly in front of all His disciples so they could hear Him. They all knew Peter had not stood faithfully as a rock. What had turned Simon's name to "Peter the rock" was when Simon received the revelation that Jesus was indeed the Messiah. *"And Simon Peter answered and said, Thou art the Christ, the Son of the living God. And Jesus answered and said unto him, Blessed art thou, Simon Barjona: for flesh and blood hath not revealed it unto thee, but my Father which is in heaven. And I say also unto thee, That thou art Peter, and upon this rock I will build my church; and the gates of hell shall not prevail against it"* (Matthew 16:16-18).

But look at how Peter boasted in his own strength at the Last Supper. *"Simon Peter said unto him, Lord, whither goest thou? Jesus answered him, Whither I go, thou canst not follow me now; but thou shalt follow me afterwards. Peter said unto him, Lord, why cannot I follow thee now?* **I will lay down my life for thy sake**" (John 13:36-37). *"Peter answered and said unto him, Though all men shall be offended because of thee,* **yet will I never be offended**" (Matthew 26:33).

DO YOU LOVE ME MORE THAN THESE?

Consider this statement: loving Jesus is simply loving obedience! Jesus said in John 14:15, *"If ye love me, keep my commandments."* Jesus knew if Peter was to lead the other disciples and the early church, he needed to be restored. Although Peter had forsaken Christ, Jesus had not forsaken him. Jesus initiated the conversation with Peter because nobody else was talking. Jesus got straight to the point with Peter, *"lovest thou me more than these?"* Did Jesus mean, did Peter love Him more than the boats, nets, and fishing or was He talking about more than the other disciples? He was talking about both because Peter savored the things of men more than the things of God at one point. Jesus rebuked him for this earlier in Matthew 16:23, *"But he turned, and said unto Peter, Get thee behind me, Satan: thou art an offence unto me:* **for thou savourest not the things that be of God, but those that be of men.**"

Look closely at Peter's reply when Jesus asked him if he loved Him more than these, *"He saith unto him, Yea, Lord; thou knowest that I love thee"* (John 21:15). Something interesting here is the Greek words for love. Jesus uses the word *agape*—the highest love of the will, love that implies total commitment. Peter answered back by using the Greek word *phileo*, a brotherly love, but not a total commitment. Peter was possibly thinking of his denials and disobedience. He may have felt too guilty to claim the same type of love toward Jesus. I can see Peter holding his head low to even say the word phileo.

Jesus then commissioned Peter, *"Feed my lambs."* This is the same responsibility Jesus gives to every minister of the Gospel. *"Take heed therefore unto yourselves, and to all the flock, over the which the Holy Ghost hath made you overseers, to **feed the church of God**, which he hath purchased with his own blood"* (Acts 20:28). Peter himself exhorted overseers later in his epistle, ***"Feed the flock of God** which is among you, taking the oversight thereof, not by constraint, but willingly; not for filthy lucre, but of a ready mind"* (1 Peter 5:2). Jesus continued to show the greater love (agape) to Peter in the next verse. *"He saith to him again the second time, Simon, son of Jonas, lovest thou me? He saith unto him, Yea, Lord; thou knowest that I love thee. He saith unto him, Feed my sheep"* (John 21:16). Jesus was teaching Peter and not reminding him of his failures. He knew Peter was fully aware of his failures. Once again, a second time, Jesus uses the word agape, and Peter once again feeling unworthy to use that word replies with the word *phileo*. Jesus charged Peter again, *"Feed my sheep."*

Jesus still wasn't through with Peter. There is one more question in the next verse. *"He saith unto him the third time, Simon, son of Jonas, lovest thou me? Peter was grieved because he said unto him the third time, Lovest thou me? And he said unto him, Lord, thou knowest all things; thou knowest that I love thee. Jesus saith unto him, Feed my sheep"* (John 21:17). This time Peter was grieved when Jesus uses a different word for love. Unlike the first two questions, this time Jesus used the word for love phileo. Peter's heart broke and Peter responded this time with, *"Lord, thou knowest all things; thou knowest that I love thee."* His response was again with the word p*hileo*. At least Peter was honest. Peter's restoration was complete, but Jesus was still not through with Peter.

After this day, the Apostle Peter remained obedient to the Lord's commission for the rest of his life. Peter finally had true agape love for Jesus. He wrote about it in 1 Peter 1:5-9, *"Who are kept by the power of God through faith unto salvation ready to be revealed in the last time. Wherein ye greatly rejoice, though now for a season, if need be, ye are in heaviness through manifold temptations: That the trial of your faith, being much more precious than of gold that perisheth, though it be tried with fire, might be found unto praise and honour and glory at the appearing of Jesus Christ: Whom **having not seen, ye love**; in whom, though now ye see him not, yet believing, ye rejoice with joy unspeakable and full of glory: Receiving the end of your faith, even the salvation of your souls."* In verse 8, the word Peter used for love is *agape*. This divine love (the highest form of love) came to Peter when he received the Holy Spirit.

Peter finally had true "agape" love for Jesus.

Notice also that Jesus first said to Peter, *"feed my* **lambs**.*"* Then He said, *"feed my* **sheep***"* the next two times. The Greek words are also different here. "Lambs" is from a Greek word indicating a lambkin or a baby lamb. "Sheep" is from a Greek word indicating a mature or aged sheep. This shows a growth process. Peter was once a lamb (a baby) in spiritual things, but later became a seasoned veteran of the faith. Jesus was showing him that he was going through a growth process personally and, due to his experience, he would eventually be able to help other believers in their growth process. No wonder he later wrote, *"But **grow in grace**, and in the knowledge of our Lord and Saviour Jesus Christ"* (2 Peter 3:18). Be patient with yourself and with others because we are all growing in our faith.

JESUS PROPHESIES PETER'S MARTYRDOM

Now, let's look at John 21:18-19, *"Verily, verily, I say unto thee, When thou wast young, thou girdest thyself, and walkedst whither thou wouldest: but when thou shalt be old, thou shalt stretch forth thy hands, and another shall gird thee, and carry thee whither thou wouldest not. This spake he, signifying by what death he should glorify God. And when he had spoken this, he saith unto him, Follow me."* Jesus was telling Peter here, "you are going to get old and you are going to be crucified for your faith and testimony." John was also explaining to us that Jesus was telling Peter that he was going to glorify God as a martyr. Herod ordered James to be killed with the sword and planned to do the same to Peter, but God intervened (Acts 12:1-3). *"And when Herod would have brought him forth, the same night Peter was sleeping between two soldiers, bound with two chains: and the keepers before the door kept the prison. And, behold, the angel of the Lord came upon him, and a light shined in the prison: and he smote Peter on the side, and raised him up, saying, Arise up quickly. And his chains fell off from his hands. And the angel said unto him, Gird thyself, and bind on thy sandals. And so he did. And he saith unto him, Cast thy garment about thee, and follow me"* (Acts 12:6-8). You might be thinking how could Peter sleep knowing that Herod was going to kill him in the morning? It's because Peter had a promise from the Lord that he would grow old and at this time Peter wasn't old yet. Church Tradition says that Peter was crucified in Rome and he requested to be crucified upside down because he didn't feel worthy to die in the same manner as the Lord. By the time John had written this Gospel, Peter had already been martyred.

Sometimes we are taught to look at death as defeat, but Paul spoke of death as a victory to the believer in 1 Corinthians 15:54-57, *"So when this corruptible shall have put on incorruption, and this mortal shall have put on immortality, then shall be brought to pass the saying that is written,* **Death is swallowed up in victory**. *O death, where is thy sting? O grave, where is thy victory? The sting of death is sin; and the strength of sin is the law. But thanks be to God,* **which giveth us the victory through our Lord Jesus Christ**.*"* The grave or death has no victory over a child of God. Jesus spoke to Peter of his own cross in John 21:19, and then Jesus spoke these words to Peter, "Follow me." Jesus repeated the same call for Peter to follow Him that he gave him over three years earlier. So, our initial calling is our continual calling—to "follow Him." Jesus had restored Peter to ministry completely and Peter accepted this fully.

Even though there was more work to do on Peter, he asked Jesus about John's calling and future in John 21:20-23: *"Then Peter, turning about, seeth the disciple whom Jesus loved following; which also leaned on his breast at supper, and said, Lord, which is he that betrayeth thee? Peter seeing him saith to Jesus, Lord, and what shall this man do? Jesus saith unto him, If I will that he tarry till I come, what is that to thee? follow thou me. Then went this saying abroad among the brethren, that that disciple should not die: yet Jesus said not unto him, He shall not die; but, If I will that he tarry till I come, what is that to thee?"* We so quickly take our eyes off of Jesus and begin to look around at others. Peter had done this before. Remember, he took his eyes off Jesus and focused on the storm instead and sank. *"And he said, Come. And when Peter was come down out of the ship, he walked on the water, to go to Jesus.* **But when he saw the wind boisterous**, **he was afraid**; *and beginning to sink, he cried, saying, Lord, save me. And immediately Jesus stretched forth his hand, and caught him, and said unto him, O thou of little faith, wherefore didst thou doubt?"* (Matthew 14:29-31) Peter saw John and asked Jesus, "Lord, and what shall this man do?" Isn't that the way we are? If God speaks something to us, we worry about what He is going to make others do. Jesus replied back to Peter in John 21:22, **"If I will that he tarry till I come**, **what is that to thee**? **follow thou me."** In other words, "Peter, My will for John is none of your business." Jesus was saying, "Peter, you take care of Peter and I will take care of John."

Whatever made Peter think this way was changed by the Holy Spirit because Peter and John worked together in unity after Pentecost. *"Now Peter and John went up together into the temple at the hour of prayer, being the ninth hour. And a certain man lame from his mother's womb was carried, whom they laid daily at the gate of the temple which is called Beautiful, to ask alms of them that entered into the temple; Who seeing Peter and John about to go into the temple asked an alms. And Peter, fastening his eyes upon him with John, said, Look on us. And he gave heed unto*

> Peter and John worked together in unity after Pentecost.

them, expecting to receive something of them. Then Peter said, Silver and gold have I none; but such as I have give I thee: In the name of Jesus Christ of Nazareth rise up and walk. And he took him by the right hand, and lifted him up: and immediately his feet and ankle bones received strength. And he leaping up stood, and walked, and entered with them into the temple, walking, and leaping, and praising God. And all the people saw him walking and praising God: And they knew that it was he which sat for alms at the Beautiful gate of the temple: and they were filled with wonder and amazement at that which had happened unto him. And as the lame man which was healed held Peter and John, all the people ran together unto them in the porch that is called Solomon's, greatly wondering"* (Acts 3:1-11). After Pentecost, you see Peter, John, and the Holy Spirit walking in one accord as a dynamic ministry team.

Let's move on to John 21:24-25, *"This is the disciple which testifieth of these things, and wrote these things: and we know that his testimony is true. And there are also many other things which Jesus did, the which, if they should be written every one, I suppose that even the world itself could not contain the books that should be written. Amen."* A rumor started circulated that John would never die. *"Then went this saying abroad among the brethren, that that disciple should not die: yet Jesus said not unto him, He shall not die; but, If I will that he tarry till I come, what is that to thee?"* (John 21:23). Jesus' words had been misunderstood to mean John would not die. John survived all the other apostles and was eventually exiled to the Island of Patmos. He escaped all the dangers of persecution and later lived a peaceful life as the Bishop of Ephesus. He eventually died at close to one hundred years old, the only apostle to die of old age. He wrote in John 21:24, *"This is the disciple which testifieth of these things, and wrote these things: and we know that his testimony is true."* John was correcting the misunderstanding before his death.

John 21:25 speaks for itself, *"And there are also many other things which Jesus did, the which, if they should be written every one, I suppose that even the world itself could not contain the books that should be written. Amen."* Throughout the Gospel of John, he presents the Lord Jesus Christ as Almighty God. He portrayed Christ as the Word made flesh who dwelled among us, who was despised and rejected, yet He loved His Father fully. And Jesus loved us enough to go to the cross and pay our sin debt in full. Only His sinless, righteous blood could redeem mankind from their sins. John and all the other New Testament writers only gave us a small fraction of all Jesus said and did during His thirty-three years on Earth. He always spent His time doing good. *"How God anointed Jesus of Nazareth with the Holy Ghost and with power:* **who went about doing good***, and healing all that were oppressed of the devil; for God was with him"* (Acts 10:38). Jesus as a man humbled Himself and did only those things He heard from His heavenly Father. He worked the works of God through the mighty power of the indwelling Holy Spirit. These writers of the New Testament only scratched the surface of all Jesus did for us. The world could not contain the books that should be written of all the words and works of Jesus. Amen!

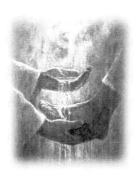

CHAPTER 11

THE KINGDOM OF GOD
(Acts 1)

The book of Acts has come to be called "Acts of the Apostles," but it was originally called the "Acts of Jesus Christ through His servants." *"The former treatise have I made, O Theophilus, of all that Jesus began both to do and teach"* (Acts 1:1). The former treatise means a "word" or "discourse." The word "former" actually means "first" book, which is referring to the book of Luke. It was also addressed to Theophilus. Who was Theophilus? There are several different theories, but the simple fact is we do not know exactly who he was. The name "Theophilus" literally means "lover of God," but carries the idea of a "friend of God." Some believe this was a generic title that applies to all Christians. I personally believe both, there must have been an individual named Theophilus because Luke addressed Him as "most excellent Theophilus" in his first book (Gospel). *"It seemed good to me also, having had perfect understanding of all things from the very first, to write unto thee in order, **most excellent Theophilus**, That thou mightest know the certainty of those things, wherein thou hast been instructed"* (Luke 1:3-4). At one time, the Gospel of Luke and the book of the Acts of Jesus Christ were joined together as one book with two volumes. The book of Luke was volume one and the Acts of Jesus Christ was volume two. Look at the phrase "all that Jesus began to do and teach." The Gospel of Luke describes only the beginning of Jesus' work on earth. Acts describes the continuation of His work on earth through His disciples (the lovers of God). And Jesus continues that work through the Holy Spirit to our present day and beyond.

Jesus is working or giving orders to His apostles from His headquarters in heaven. To make this clearer, let us look at the word "apostle." During this time, the word "apostle" was a naval term that described an admiral, the fleet of ships that traveled with him, and the crew that accompanied the admiral. They would be sent out on missions to locate territories where the kingdom they represented did not exist. Once the region was identified, the admiral and his crew, and all their cargo and belongings would disembark and work together to colonize the region for their king. They would teach the people of the region the language, ways, and customs of their king. Their purpose was total colonization of the region. They would establish a new culture, and a new life for the people of the new region. The apostle or admiral was the team leader establishing a new society. Once they completed the task, most of the team got back on the ships, went out to find another area, and repeated the entire colonization process all over again. Some were left behind as governors and leaders of the new region.

The word "apostle" described someone who had the authority to act as an "ambassador" of the king he represented to another government. *"Now then we are **ambassadors for Christ**, as though God did beseech you by us: we pray you in Christ's stead, be ye reconciled to God. For he hath made him to be sin for us, who knew no sin; that we might be made the righteousness of God in him"* (2

Corinthians 5:20-21). An apostle was an envoy sent to do business on behalf of the one who sent him. *"For which I am an **ambassador** in bonds: that therein I may speak boldly, as I ought to speak"* (Ephesians 6:20). *"A wicked messenger falleth into mischief: but a faithful **ambassador is health** [brings healing]"* (Proverbs 13:17).

> *An apostle was an envoy sent to do business on behalf of the one who sent him.*

MANY INFALLIBLE PROOFS

Read with me Acts 1:2-3, *"Until the day in which he was taken up, after that he through the Holy Ghost had given commandments unto the apostles whom he had chosen: To whom also he shewed himself alive after his passion by **many infallible proofs**, being seen of them forty days, and speaking of the things pertaining to the kingdom of God."* Jesus was instructing the apostles what to do in His physical absence. Consider the phrase "Through the Holy Ghost had given commandments." Jesus established the fact of His resurrection with many infallible proofs during the forty days between His resurrection and His ascension. He left no doubt in their minds. I mentioned many infallible proofs in the last two chapters. The Apostle Paul mentions one of these many infallible proofs. *"After that, **he was seen of above five hundred brethren at once**; of whom the greater part remain unto this present, but some are fallen asleep"* (1 Corinthians 15:6). More than 500 people saw the resurrected Jesus and most of them were still alive twenty-five years later in Paul's days. Jesus used the forty days to speak to His apostles things pertaining to the kingdom of God.

Jesus had taught them to pray *"**Thy kingdom come**, Thy will be done in earth, as it is in heaven"* (Matthew 6:10). Jesus was teaching them how to establish His kingdom on earth. The kingdom of God is mentioned throughout the Old and New Testaments. *"But **seek ye first the kingdom of God**, and his righteousness; and all these things shall be added unto you"* (Matthew 6:33). The Lord told us to seek first His kingdom, but in the church world today, so little is known about His kingdom. Jesus reigns as King through righteousness. To seek His righteousness is to seek to be under His rulership. Jesus' reign is infinite. Jesus' reign is established in God's promises, which they are waiting for in Acts 1. Here are some things Jesus would have taught them about the kingdom of God. His kingdom would be established on earth. Jesus mentioned the kingdom of God at the Last Supper. *"Verily I say unto you, I will drink no more of the fruit of the vine, until that day that I drink it new **in the kingdom of God**"* (Mark 14:25).

Let's go back to Matthew 6:10, *"**Thy kingdom come**, Thy will be done in earth, as it is in heaven."* This is actually praying for the day when God will bring heaven to earth. God still has a plan for this planet called earth. He will rule and reign here along with all believers when He returns. When you submit to His lordship, it is not about rules and regulations, but "righteousness, peace, and joy in the Holy Ghost." Paul explained, *"For the kingdom of God is not meat and drink; but righteousness, and peace, and joy in the Holy Ghost"* (Romans 14:17). In other words, the kingdom is not about observing dead rituals and ceremonies, but about enjoying a vibrant relationship with God through the Holy Spirit. The greatest prayer we can pray is for His kingdom to come.

THE KINGDOM OF GOD (Acts 1)

Read these scriptures about the kingdom, *"But if I with the finger of God cast out devils, no doubt **the kingdom of God is come upon you**"* (Luke 11:20). A kingdom is a king's domain, the boundaries wherein a king rules. So, Jesus brought the kingdom of God down to earth with Him. *"But into whatsoever city ye enter, and they receive you not, go your ways out into the streets of the same, and say, Even the very dust of your city, which cleaveth on us, we do wipe off against you: notwithstanding be ye sure of this, that **the kingdom of God is come nigh unto you**"* (Luke 10:10-11).

You might ask, "how was the kingdom near them?" The answer is the kingdom was near them because Jesus, the King, was there among them. Through the cross, Jesus inaugurated His Father's kingdom. He used His disciples, which includes us, to consummate it. Jesus is not going to become King; He already is King over Heaven and Earth. *"And Jesus came and spake unto them, saying, All power is given unto me in heaven and in earth"* (Matthew 28:18). It is our responsibility as the church to make the invisible kingdom visible. The only way the kingdom of God can be manifested is by the way we, His citizens, live. Philippians 3:20 says, *"For our conversation is in heaven; from whence also we look for the Saviour, the Lord Jesus Christ."*

> The only way the kingdom of God can be manifested is by the way we, His citizens, live.

*"And, being assembled together with them, commanded them that they should not depart from Jerusalem, but **wait for the promise of the Father**, which, saith he, ye have heard of me. For John truly baptized with water;*

but ye shall be baptized with the Holy Ghost not many days hence" (Acts 1:4-5). Notice they were all assembled together. Jesus commanded them to stay in Jerusalem. His first commission was not to go but to "wait." *"And, behold, I send the promise of my Father upon you: but **tarry ye in the city of Jerusalem, until ye be endued with power from on high**. And he led them out as far as to Bethany, and he lifted up his hands, and blessed them. And it came to pass, while he blessed them, he was parted from them, and carried up into heaven. And they worshipped him, and returned to Jerusalem with great joy: And were continually in the temple, praising and blessing God. Amen"* (Luke 24:49-53). They were to tarry (wait or stay) at Jerusalem for ten days and not depart. I have always thought they stayed in the upper room and did not come out. *"And when they were come in, **they went up into an upper room**, where abode both Peter, and James, and John, and Andrew, Philip, and Thomas, Bartholomew, and Matthew, James the son of Alphaeus, and Simon Zelotes, and Judas the brother of James"* (Acts 1:13). But the Bible doesn't indicate that. In fact, Luke 24:53 informs us that they *"**were continually in the temple**, praising and blessing God."* They were no longer hiding but waiting in the Temple and the upper room before they preached the kingdom of God to every creature.

Now we move on to Acts 1:6-7, *"When they therefore were come together, they asked of him, saying, Lord, **wilt thou at this time restore again the kingdom to Israel**? And he said unto them, It is not for you to know the times or the seasons, which the Father hath put in his own power."* They were still focused on a natural kingdom instead of the spiritual kingdom. I believe He will restore Israel. After nearly 2,000 years of not being a nation, geographical Israel became a nation again in 1948, which is a sign of the end times. The apostles were most likely thinking about Daniel 7:27, *"And the kingdom and dominion, and the greatness of the kingdom under the whole heaven, shall be given to the people of the saints of the most High, whose kingdom is an everlasting kingdom, and all dominions shall serve and obey him."* I want you to see something in this verse. God's everlasting kingdom will not be in heaven only (heaven is the throne room) but "under the whole heaven" too. The earth and all the dominions of man shall serve Him. The disciples were probably also thinking of God's words to Moses in Exodus 19:5-6, *"Now therefore, if ye will obey my voice indeed, and keep my covenant, then ye shall be a peculiar treasure unto me above all people: for all the earth is mine: And ye shall be unto me* **a kingdom of priests, and an holy nation***. These are the words which thou shalt speak unto the children of Israel."*

GOD'S PURPOSE FOR GOVERNMENT

We all need some form of government in our lives. God established government to maintain order in society. Otherwise, you would have total chaos. Government has been an important concern since the first Adam when God blessed him. *"And God blessed them, and God said unto them, Be fruitful, and multiply, and replenish the earth, and subdue it:* **and have dominion** *over the fish of the sea, and over the fowl of the air, and over every living thing that moveth upon the earth"* (Genesis 1:28). Neither Adam nor Israel kept their covenant with God. Adam rejected God's rule and so did Israel because they did not want God to rule over them; they wanted to rule themselves. As a result, they lost their dominion. *"And the Lord* *said unto Samuel, Hearken unto the voice of the people in all that they say unto thee: for they have not rejected thee,* **but they have rejected me, that I should not reign over them**" (1 Samuel 8:7). Don't be too harsh on Israel; America has done the same thing. The test of government is to whose rule will you submit. There are two choices God's or Satan's? The devil's temptations of Jesus were the same test over government in Matthew 4 and Luke 4. Pause and go read it with this in mind.

Jesus' answer to the disciples' question about restoring the kingdom to Israel in verse six is found in verse seven, *"When they therefore were come together, they asked of him, saying, Lord, wilt thou at this time restore again the kingdom to Israel? And he said unto them, It is not for you to know the times or the seasons, which the Father hath put in his own power"* (Acts 1:6-7). Jesus was saying even though you may be interested in this, it's not for you to know. In His first coming, Jesus came to establish a spiritual kingdom in the hearts of people (Luke 17:21). When He comes again, He will usher in a literal kingdom that will rule over all the earth and we will reign as kings and priests with Him forever (Revelation 1:6; 11:15; 19:11-16; 20:6; 22:5).

Jesus went on in to say in Acts 1:8, *"But ye shall receive power, after that the Holy Ghost is come upon you: and ye shall be witnesses unto me both in Jerusalem, and in all Judaea, and in Samaria, and unto the uttermost part of the earth."* The Greek word translated "power" in this verse is dunamis which has the meaning of authority. In fact, it's the same word from which we derive the English words "dynamic" and "dynamite." The purpose of the baptism of the Holy Spirit is to receive supernatural power and authority to be dynamic witnesses for Christ. When you get saved, you receive the indwelling presence of His Spirit, but you don't receive the full power and authority of the Spirit until you are baptized in the Holy Spirit.

Acts 1:9 indicates these were the Lord's final words before His ascension, *"And when he had spoken these things, while they beheld, **he was taken up; and a cloud received him out of their sight**."* Luke 24:48-52 lets us know that these were words of blessing. Jesus was passing the torch on to His disciples. *"And ye are witnesses of these things. And, behold, I send the promise of my Father upon you: but tarry ye in the city of Jerusalem, until ye be endued with power from on high. And he led them out as far as to Bethany, and he lifted up his hands, and **blessed them**. And it came to pass, while **he blessed them**, he was parted from them, and carried up into heaven. And they worshipped him, and returned to Jerusalem with great joy."*

The disciples certainly fulfilled this next verse after Pentecost, *"And ye shall be witnesses unto me both in Jerusalem, and in all Judaea, and in Samaria, and unto the uttermost part of the earth"* (Acts 1:8). Some have called it the table of contents for the book of Acts. Reading through Acts, it becomes clear. The Gospel was preached in Jerusalem in chapters 1-7, it was preached in Judea and Samaria in chapters 13-18, and then it was taken to the uttermost parts of the earth in chapters 19-28. I must note this here, the apostles were looking for the restoration of the kingdom in Israel. Many today say God is finished with Israel and that all His promises were transferred to the church (also known as replacement theology). Jesus didn't say He had no plans for Israel, but He refocused their attention to His plan for them at that present time. Clearly, God is not finished with Israel.

For the apostles and for Luke, the ascension of Jesus was extremely important. Luke ended his first volume, the Gospel of Luke, with the ascension and began with it in his second volume, the Acts of Jesus Christ (Luke 24:51, Acts 1:9). As Jesus was carried up to heaven, the disciples worshipped Him. They traveled back to Jerusalem (about two miles from Bethany) with great joy. They were regularly in the temple, praising and blessing God. It was a much different reaction than when He was placed into the tomb. Their sorrow was turned to joy. They were finally realizing the benefits that would come because Jesus was going back to the Father. Their worship was a sign they believed the promises of Jesus. But first, Angels appeared to remind them of their assignment, *"And while they looked stedfastly toward heaven as he went up, behold, two men stood by them in white apparel; Which also said, Ye men of Galilee, why stand ye gazing up into heaven? this same Jesus, which is taken up from you into heaven, shall so come in like manner as ye have seen him go into heaven. Then returned they unto Jerusalem from the mount called Olivet, which is from Jerusalem a sabbath day's journey"* (Acts 1:10-12). When Jesus ascended, the payment for sin was confirmed that the debt was paid in full! The New Covenant was sealed by His blood and confirmed by His ascension.

Hebrews 10:10-14 explains Jesus' once and for all sacrifice, *"By the which will we are sanctified through the offering of the body of Jesus Christ **once for all**. And every priest standeth daily ministering and offering oftentimes the same sacrifices, which can never take away sins: But this man, after he had offered **one sacrifice for sins for ever**, sat down on the right hand of God; From henceforth expecting till his enemies be made* *his footstool.* **For by one offering** *he hath perfected for ever them that are sanctified."* A New Covenant began. When Jesus ascended to the throne (the Mercy Seat), the intercessory work of Christ on our behalf began. *"My little children, these things write I unto you, that ye sin not. And if any man sin,* **we have an advocate with the Father, Jesus Christ the righteous**.*"* (1 John 2:1). *"Who is he that condemneth? It is Christ that died, yea rather, that is risen again, who is even at the right hand of God,* **who also maketh intercession for us**" (Romans 8:34). *"Wherefore he is able also to save them to the uttermost that come unto God by him, seeing* **he ever liveth to make intercession for them**" (Hebrews 7:25).

Clearly, Jesus is actively working on our behalf even now. Jesus is interceding for us while Satan, whose name means "accuser," is accusing us day and night. He is pointing out all our sins and weaknesses to God and to us. But we have to put it under the blood. The Judge, who is now our heavenly Father, declares our debt is paid in full. "For he hath made him to be sin for us, who knew no sin; that we might be made the righteousness of God in him" (2 Corinthians 5:21). The disciples knew by this time what this following verse meant. *"For there is one God, and one mediator between God and men, the man Christ Jesus"* (1 Timothy 2:5). Jesus Christ is the perfect man. He was fully man and fully God. He had to take that earthly body of a man into heaven, which still exists and send back the spiritual "man" (Holy Spirit) to live in us. Some today don't believe in the physical return of the Lord, but I disagree. Remember, the angels said right after His ascension, *"This same Jesus, which is taken up from you into heaven, shall so come in like manner as ye have seen him go into heaven"* (Acts 1:11). Plus, Jesus promised, *"I go to* prepare a place for you. And if I go and prepare a place for you, **I will come again**, and receive you unto myself; that where I am, there ye may be also" (John 14:2-3).

Here is Peter's explanation of the lame man's healing in Acts 3:12-21, "And when Peter saw it, he answered unto the people, Ye men of Israel, why marvel ye at this? or why look ye so earnestly on us, as though by our own power or holiness we had made this man to walk? The God of Abraham, and of Isaac, and of Jacob, the God of our fathers, hath glorified his Son Jesus; whom ye delivered up, and denied him in the presence of Pilate, when he was determined to let him go. But ye denied the Holy One and the Just, and desired a murderer to be granted unto you; And killed the Prince of life, whom God hath raised from the dead; whereof we are witnesses. And his name through faith in his name hath made this man strong, whom ye see and know: yea, the faith which is by him hath given him this perfect soundness in the presence of you all. And now, brethren, I wot that through ignorance ye did it, as did also your rulers. But those things, which God before had shewed by the mouth of all his prophets, that Christ should suffer, he hath so fulfilled. Repent ye therefore, and be converted, that your sins may be blotted out, when the times of refreshing shall come from the presence of the Lord. And he shall send Jesus Christ, which before was preached unto you: Whom the heaven must receive until the times of restitution of all things, which God hath spoken by the mouth of all his holy prophets since the world began."

Also read Acts 1:13, "And when they were come in, **they went up into an upper room**, where abode both Peter, and James, and John, and Andrew, Philip, and Thomas, Bartholomew, and Matthew, James the son of

Alphaeus, and Simon Zelotes, and Judas the brother of James." Two angels told the disciples Jesus would return the same way they saw Him go. The disciples followed Jesus' command and waited in Jerusalem for the gift of the Holy Spirit. They spent the time in prayer in one accord. *"These all **continued with one accord in prayer and supplication**, with the women, and Mary the mother of Jesus, and with his brethren"* (Acts 1:14). The word "abode" in verse thirteen implies that they were in the upper room for ten days until Pentecost.

THE IMPORTANCE OF WAITING ON THE LORD

So, the upper room became a waiting room. Waiting goes against our flesh. Waiting upon the Lord would soon become their lifestyle. The Apostle Paul learned this very important lesson in ministry and taught others to do the same, *"Or ministry, **let us wait on our ministering**: or he that teacheth, on teaching; Or he that exhorteth, on exhortation: he that giveth, let him do it with simplicity; he that ruleth, with diligence; he that sheweth mercy, with cheerfulness. Let love be without dissimulation. Abhor that which is evil; cleave to that which is good"* (Romans 12:7-9). We have all been in God's waiting room. Have you ever been waiting for the doctor (someone who is going to try to help you) in a waiting room with other people? How did you use your time waiting for the doctor? Will you use your time sleeping? People fall asleep while waiting. Some are the "eyeball rollers." Every time another patient is called, they roll

> *Waiting upon the Lord would soon become their lifestyle.*

their eyes. Then there are the complainers because the doctor is taking too long. When I go to the doctor, I come prepared to wait. When waiting becomes your lifestyle, worry leaves, and the peace of God comes. Paul knew this secret, *"Be careful for nothing; but in every thing by prayer and supplication with thanksgiving let your requests be made known unto God. And the peace of God, which passeth all understanding, shall keep your hearts and minds through Christ Jesus"* (Philippians 4:6-7).

Talk and listen to God in the waiting room. Keep your mind stayed on the Lord in the waiting room. This waiting room was a crowded place. Remember, if we are in a waiting room, we are all waiting for the same purpose, to see the doctor. The Bible assures us of the benefits of waiting. *"But they that wait upon the Lord shall renew their strength; they shall mount up with wings as eagles; they shall run, and not be weary; and they shall walk, and not faint"* (Isaiah 40:31). The word "renew" means to "exchange" in this scripture. You exchange your weakness for His strength in waiting. Psalms 25:4-6 says, *"Shew me thy ways, O Lord; teach me thy paths. Lead me in thy truth, and teach me: for thou art the God of my salvation;* **on thee do I wait all the day**. *Remember, O Lord, thy tender mercies and thy lovingkindnesses; for they have been ever of old."*

In waiting, we learn the ways of the Lord. In waiting, we learn the difference between our ways and His ways. Isaiah 55:7-9 declares, *"Let the wicked forsake his way, and the unrighteous man his thoughts: and let him return unto the Lord, and he will have mercy upon him; and to our God, for he will abundantly pardon. For my thoughts are not your thoughts, neither are your ways my ways, saith the Lord. For as the heavens are higher than* the earth, so are my ways higher than your ways, and my thoughts than your thoughts." In waiting, He will teach us His paths. His path is a lifestyle of waiting on Him. *"Thou wilt shew me the path of life: in thy presence is fulness of joy; at thy right hand there are pleasures for evermore"* (Psalms 16:11). While they waited for the Holy Spirit, they were learning to follow truth.

There are many Psalms which encourage waiting upon God:

- Psalms 4:4-5—*"Stand in awe, and sin not: commune with your own heart upon your bed, and* **be still**. *Selah. Offer the sacrifices of righteousness, and put your trust in the Lord."*

- Psalm 25:3-5—*"Yea,* **let none that wait on thee be ashamed***: let them be ashamed which transgress without cause. Shew me thy ways, O LORD; teach me thy paths. Lead me in thy truth, and teach me: for thou art the God of my salvation;* **on thee do I wait all the day***."*

- Psalms 27:13-14—*"I had fainted, unless I had believed to see the goodness of the Lord in the land of the living.* **Wait on the Lord***: be of good courage, and he shall strengthen thine heart:* **wait, I say, on the Lord***."*

- Psalm 37:7-9—*"Rest in the Lord, and* **wait patiently for him***: fret not thyself because of him who prospereth in his way, because of the man who bringeth wicked devices to pass. Cease from anger, and forsake wrath: fret not thyself in any wise to do evil. For evildoers shall be cut off:* **but those that wait upon the LORD, they shall inherit the earth***."*

- Psalms 37:34—"**Wait on the Lord**, and keep his way, and he shall exalt thee to inherit the land: when the wicked are cut off, thou shalt see it."

- Psalms 52:9—"I will praise thee for ever, because thou hast done it: and **I will wait on thy name**; for it is good before thy saints."

- Psalms 62:1-2, 5—"Truly **my soul waiteth upon God**: from him cometh my salvation. He only is my rock and my salvation; he is my defence; I shall not be greatly moved … My soul, **wait thou only upon God**; for my expectation is from him."

- Psalms 130:5-6—"**I wait for the Lord, my soul doth wait,** and in his word do I hope. **My soul waiteth for the Lord more than they that watch for the morning**: I say, more than they that watch for the morning."

If you jumped ahead of these verses to see what I would say next, go back. You haven't learned to wait yet. Remember what you are waiting for in each scripture I wrote: In Psalms 27, we learn the goodness and courage of the Lord. In Psalms 37, we learn to inherit the land and find strength to keep His ways. In Psalms 52, we learn His name. In Psalms 62, there is solitude and stability in waiting. By waiting, He becomes my rock, my shield, and my salvation. In Psalms 130, while waiting, we find hope in His Word. Waiting makes us alert and sensitive as to when God is speaking to us and directing us as a watchman. Psalms 147 lets us know God doesn't take pleasure in what we do in our own strength. Favor comes to those who wait on the Lord.

While the disciples were waiting in the upper room,

Peter, as the leader, received insight into the Scriptures. *"And in those days Peter stood up in the midst of the disciples, and said, (the number of names together were about an hundred and twenty,) Men and brethren, this scripture must needs have been fulfilled, which the Holy Ghost by the mouth of David spake before concerning Judas, which was guide to them that took Jesus. For he was numbered with us, and had obtained part of this ministry. Now this man purchased a field with the reward of iniquity; and falling headlong, he burst asunder in the midst, and all his bowels gushed out. And it was known unto all the dwellers at Jerusalem; insomuch as that field is called in their proper tongue, Aceldama, that is to say, The field of blood. For it is written in the book of Psalms, Let his habitation be desolate, and let no man dwell therein: and his bishoprick let another take"* (Acts 1:15-20).

Peter's purpose in addressing the disciples and others is to explain Judas' treachery and death in order to encourage them to choose a replacement for Judas. Some may have doubted what Peter said in verse 16. Peter mentioned the Holy Spirit spoke by the mouth of David, concerning Judas. In verse 20, Peter quoted from Psalms 69:25, *"Let their habitation be desolate; and let none dwell in their tents"* and Psalms 109:8, *"Let their habitation be desolate; and let none dwell in their tents."* Peter was led by the Holy Spirit to remember these verses. Peter understood something he had always missed. The fulfillment of Scripture was important.

In John 13:18, Jesus quoted Psalms 41:9, *"I speak not of you all: I know whom I have chosen: but that the scripture may be fulfilled, He that eateth bread with me hath lifted up his heel against me."* This was speaking of Judas walking away from Jesus and Judas' betrayal. To lift up your heel, in their custom, was to walk away permanently. To show your heel to someone was a great insult. Peter, James, and John were close enough to hear Jesus pray, *"While I was with them in the world, I kept them in thy name: those that thou gavest me I have kept, and none of them is lost, but the son of perdition; that the scripture might be fulfilled"* (John 17:12). Judas' betrayal was the fulfillment of Scripture. Peter, in seeking the fulfillment of Psalms 109:8, said, "Let his days be few; and let another take his office." He established the essential criteria for the one who would replace Judas as an apostle—he must be someone who had been an active disciple from beginning of Jesus' ministry till His ascension. *"Wherefore of these men which have companied with us all the time that the Lord Jesus went in and out among us, Beginning from the baptism of John, unto that same day that he was taken up from us, must one be ordained to be a witness with us of his resurrection"* (Acts 1:21-22).

They chose two candidates. The first was Joseph, known as Barsabas (which means "son of the sabbath"), whose surname was Justus. The second man was Matthias. Up to this point, we have not heard of either of these men. Tradition says Matthias served later in Ethiopia. *"And they prayed, and said, Thou, Lord, which knowest the hearts of all men, shew whether of these two thou hast chosen, that he may take part of this ministry and apostleship, from which Judas by transgression fell, that he might go to his own place. And they gave for their lots; and the lot fell upon Matthias; and he was numbered with the eleven apostles"* (Acts 1:24-26).

They all prayed together. In their prayer, they first acknowledged that they did not know everyone's heart. So, they asked the One who knows everyone's heart to show them which of the two He had chosen. God does not look at the outward appearance, but on the heart. They asked God Himself to choose. Who is to take part in this ministry and apostleship? Mathias, whose name means "gift of God," was the choice made by the disciples giving forth their lots. Their vote was not a gamble but the same way they selected representatives later at the Jerusalem Council. We see this in Acts 15:25-28, *"It seemed good unto us, being assembled with one accord, to send chosen men unto you with our beloved Barnabas and Paul, Men that have hazarded their lives for the name of our Lord Jesus Christ. We have sent therefore Judas and Silas, who shall also tell you the same things by mouth. For it seemed good to the Holy Ghost, and to us, to lay upon you no greater burden than these necessary things."* James evaluated this new work of God among the Gentiles just as any work should be judged. James looked at what was written and quoted from Amos 9:11-12, *"In that day will I raise up the tabernacle of David that is fallen, and close up the breaches thereof; and I will raise up his ruins, and I will build it as in the days of old: That they may possess the remnant of Edom, and of all the heathen, which are called by my name, saith the Lord that doeth this."* Peter and James both looked to scriptures for the answer.

Where did they learn this? In the upper room while waiting on the Promise of the Holy Spirit. Acts 2:1 states, *"And when the day of Pentecost was fully come, they were all with one accord in one place."* After the decision, they remained in one accord. Even Joseph, who was not chosen, stayed in unity. We can learn much here. I love the phrase in Acts 15:28 *"For it seemed good to the Holy Ghost, and to us, to lay upon you no greater burden than these necessary things."* Notice the phrase "It seemed good to the Holy Ghost, and to us." I have lived my life by this statement, knowing that the Holy Spirit is concerned about how I think and feel about decisions and I should be equally concerned how He feels and thinks about a matter. We must make decisions in cooperation with the Holy Spirit and one another. To be in one accord, we must first be in unity with the Word of God (Scripture) and with the Holy Spirit. Then we will have true harmony with one another. The Word and the Spirit is what brings us together in one accord. They learned in Acts 1 how to handle situations like this found in Acts 15 and they were able to keep unity with each other and the Holy Spirit. God won't bless strife, but He blesses and anoints unity among His people as David expressed in Psalm 133:1-3, *"Behold, how good and how pleasant it is* **for brethren to dwell together in unity**! *It is like the precious ointment upon the head, that ran down upon the beard, even Aaron's beard: that went down to the skirts of his garments; As the dew of Hermon, and as the dew that descended upon the mountains of Zion: for there the Lord commanded the blessing, even life for evermore."*

> *The Word and the Spirit is what brings us together in one accord.*

CHAPTER 12

PENTECOST AND BEYOND
(Acts 2)

The meaning of Pentecost is God equipping His church with His Spirit so that He will be glorified among the nations. The purpose of Pentecost is to fulfil God's mission for the world. *"For the earth shall be filled with the knowledge of the glory of the Lord, as the waters cover the sea"* (Habakkuk 2:14). If we truly understand Pentecost, our heart's desire will be burning to see every tribe, tongue, and nation bowing before the exalted Lord Jesus Christ. God's plan for being glorified among the nations started with the formation of the church. The Day of Pentecost was the birthday of the New Testament church. If our heart is not on world missions, then our heart is not in tune with God's heart. To have His heart for the nations, we must have the Holy Spirit and walk in unity. Acts 2:1-4 describes what transpired in the upper room, *"And when the day of Pentecost was fully come, they were all with one accord in one place. And suddenly there came a sound from heaven as of a rushing mighty wind, and it filled all the house where they were sitting. And there appeared unto them cloven tongues like as of fire, and it sat upon each of them. And they were all filled with the Holy Ghost, and began to speak with other tongues, as the Spirit gave them utterance."*

This was the initial experience of the infilling of the Holy Spirit on the Day of Pentecost. The word "Pentecost" means "fifty" or "fiftieth" because it occurred fifty days after Passover. The original Pentecost happened at Mount Sinai (Exodus 19 and 20) fifty days after Israel was delivered from Egypt. God instituted Pentecost as an annual festival to commemorate the giving of the law. It was a feast of the Lord held fifty days after the Feast of Passover and the combined Feast of Unleavened Bread. The first sheaf reaped from the harvest was waved unto God on the day after the Sabbath at Feast of Firstfruits. Pentecost is also called the Day of Firstfruits. *"Also in the **day of the firstfruits**, when ye bring a new meat offering unto the Lord, after your weeks be out, ye shall have an holy convocation; ye shall do no servile work."* (Numbers 28:26). On the Old Testament Day of Pentecost, Israel heard the audible voice of God speak His Law (the Ten Commandments) from Mount Sinai (Exodus 20:1-20). A few days later, they received the law written by the fiery finger of God on two tablets of stone. It is a holy law that no one can ever totally keep because we are all sinners born with a stony heart.

The law revealed to them that they were sinners in need of a savior. Ezekiel 36:26 is a prophecy about the New Covenant era, *"A new heart also will I give you, and a new spirit will I put within you: and I will take away the stony heart out of your flesh, and I will give you an heart of flesh."* This is what actually happened on the Day of Pentecost in Acts 2—Jesus put a new heart (His pure heart) and a new Spirit within them. When you receive the Holy Spirit, you are coming into a deeper covenant with the Lord. The baptism of the Holy Spirit is a token or sign of the covenant. He puts His laws in your new heart and mind. You receive Him by Grace. The Baptism of the Holy Spirit is the impartation of the Spirit of grace in its fullness.

Leviticus 23:15-22 records God's instructions concerning the Feat of Pentecost, *"And ye shall count unto you from the morrow after the sabbath, from the day that ye brought the sheaf of the wave offering; seven sabbaths shall be complete: Even unto the morrow after the seventh sabbath shall ye number fifty days; and ye shall offer a new meat offering unto the Lord. Ye shall bring out of your habitations two wave loaves of two tenth deals; they shall be of fine flour; they shall be baken with leaven; they are the firstfruits unto the Lord. And ye shall offer with the bread seven lambs without blemish of the first year, and one young bullock, and two rams: they shall be for a burnt offering unto the Lord, with their meat offering, and their drink offerings, even an offering made by fire, of sweet savour unto the Lord. Then ye shall sacrifice one kid of the goats for a sin offering, and two lambs of the first year for a sacrifice of peace offerings. And the priest shall wave them with the bread of the firstfruits for a wave offering before the Lord, with the two lambs: they shall be holy to the Lord for the priest. And ye shall proclaim on the selfsame day, that it may be an holy convocation unto you: ye shall do no servile work therein: it shall be a statute for ever in all your dwellings throughout your generations. And when ye reap the harvest of your land, thou shalt not make clean riddance of the corners of thy field when thou reapest, neither shalt thou gather any gleaning of thy harvest: thou shalt leave them unto the poor, and to the stranger: I am the Lord your God."*

There are numerous Old Testament regulations on how to celebrate Pentecost. They were to take two loaves of leavened bread and wave it before the Lord. This signified that not only will Israel be saved but a multitude of Gentiles will also come in. When the Day of Pentecost arrived, it was ten days after Jesus ascended to heaven. The disciples were still waiting in the upper room. Truly the gift of the Holy Spirit is worth waiting for. It's a phenomenal gift, not earned, but promised to all of us. *"Then Peter said unto them, Repent, and be baptized every one of you in the name of Jesus Christ for the remission of sins, and* **ye shall receive the gift of the Holy Ghost***. For the promise is unto you, and to your children, and to all that are afar off, even as many as the Lord our God shall call"* (Acts 2:38-39). It is a gift and a promise that is not earned by works but received by seeking for it.

Acts 2:1 indicates, "They were all with one accord in one place." They were in one geographical place with the same heart and love for God, and thy were waiting for the same promise. By gathering together in prayer, we realize our own weakness. They realized they could not do the task set before them without depending on one another and the power of the Holy Spirit. *"Suddenly there came a sound from heaven as of a rushing mighty wind, and it filled all the house where they were sitting"* (Acts 2:2). In the Hebrew and Greek languages, the word for "Spirit" is the same word for "breath" or "wind." The "sound from heaven" was the sound of the Holy Spirit being breathed upon and into them. It was a mighty breathing sound like in Genesis 2:7, *"And the Lord God formed man of the dust of the ground, and breathed into his nostrils the breath*

> In the Hebrew and Greek languages, the word for "Spirit" is the same word for "breath" or "wind."

of life; and man became a living soul." It is the Spirit of God as the breath or wind of God blowing life into man. In Acts, it was the Spirit of God as the breath or wind, blowing life into His new creations. We are recreated in Christ. *"Therefore if any man be in Christ, he is a new creature: old things are passed away; behold, all things are become new"* (2 Corinthians 5:17). Any man who is "in Christ," is a "new creation!" When we are baptized in the Holy Spirit, we are "in Christ" and submerged in the Holy Spirit. It is Christ in you and you in Christ. Now they could understand John 15 where the Lord said, "Abide in Me and I in you."

Read Acts 2:2 again, *"And **suddenly** there came a sound from heaven as of a rushing mighty wind, and it filled all the house where they were sitting."* This verse tells us the Holy Spirit came "suddenly." Compare that with Malachi 3:1, *"Behold, I will send my messenger, and he shall prepare the way before me: and the Lord, whom ye seek, **shall suddenly come to his temple**, even the messenger of the covenant, whom ye delight in: behold, he shall come, saith the Lord of hosts."* The "messenger of the covenant" is the Holy Spirit. Also, notice that "They were sitting" Why? Because they could not stand in the presence of the Holy Spirit. *"But who may abide the day of his coming? and **who shall stand when he appeareth**? for he is like a refiner's fire, and like fullers' soap"* (Malachi 3:2). It was a "rushing mighty wind" that came with great power. *"And there appeared unto them cloven tongues like as of fire, and it sat upon each of them"* (Acts 2:3). John the Baptist prophesied that Jesus would baptize us with the Holy Spirit and with fire. *"I indeed baptize you with water unto repentance. but he that cometh after me is mightier than I, whose shoes I am not worthy to bear:*

he shall baptize you with the Holy Ghost, **and with fire**" (Matthew 3:11). The picture of fire usually means purification like a refiner's fire purifies precious metals as Malachi 3:3 describes, *"And* **he shall sit as a refiner and purifier of silver: and he shall purify the sons of Levi, and purge them as gold and silver,** *that they may offer unto the Lord an offering in righteousness."* The Holy Spirit is not just given to us to impart His power, but also to do a work of purity in us.

The book of Malachi begins with a statement of how the covenant began, *"***I have loved you, saith the Lord***. Yet ye say, Wherein hast thou loved us? Was not Esau Jacob's brother? saith the Lord: yet I loved Jacob"* (Malachi 1:2). "I have loved you." This is what never changes about Jesus. We need to always remember that He never changes—"For I am the Lord, I change not; therefore ye sons of Jacob are not consumed" (Malachi 3:6). He loves us and that never changes. That is the only reason the refiner's fire does not consume us, but rather changes us. The Holy Spirit is a like refiner's fire to change us, to remove the dross, and to refine us as pure gold. He didn't come as a forest fire to destroy us. A life lived by faith in the Holy Spirit's fire purifies. *"That the trial of your faith,* **being much more precious than of gold that perisheth, though it be tried with fire***, might be found unto praise and honour and glory at the appearing of Jesus Christ"* (1 Peter 1:7).

James 1:2-4 tells how fiery trials have a positive purpose, *"My brethren, count it all joy when ye fall into divers temptations; Knowing this, that* **the trying of your faith worketh patience***. But let patience have her perfect work, that ye may be perfect and entire, wanting nothing."* In Romans 8:13, Paul declared, *"For if ye live after* *the flesh, ye shall die: but if ye through the Spirit do mortify the deeds of the body, ye shall live."* By yielding to the "Cloven tongues like as of fire," we are purified. A fire must have air to breath and fuel (disciples) to burn and wind to spread, and spread it did, all in one day. *"Then they that gladly received his word were baptized: and the same day there were added unto them about three thousand souls"* (Acts 2:41).

PARALLELS BETWEEN THE ORIGINAL PENTECOST AND THE ACTS 2 FULFILLMENT

Now let's look at what happened on Pentecost in Acts 2 and compare it with the original Pentecost (the giving of the Law) in Exodus 19. Hebrews 12:18-19 describes the scene at Mount Sinai, *"For ye are not come unto the mount that might be touched, and that burned with fire, nor unto blackness, and darkness, and tempest, And the sound of a trumpet, and the voice of words; which voice they that heard intreated that the word should not be spoken to them any more."* This verse mentions the supernatural phenomena that occurred at the inauguration of the Mosaic dispensation—the "fire," "tempest" (wind), and the "voice of words" (tongues). Something very similar was witnessed on Pentecost in the upper room, but without blackness or darkness, or the terror in the people. Exodus 19:16-18 describes how the fiery glory of God fell on Mount Sinai, *"And it came to pass on the third day in the morning, that there were thunders and lightnings, and a thick cloud upon the mount, and the voice of the trumpet exceeding loud; so that all the people that was in the camp trembled. And Moses brought forth the people out of the camp to meet with God; and they stood at the nether part of the mount. And mount Sinai was altogether on a smoke, because the Lord descended upon it in fire: and the smoke thereof ascended as the smoke of a furnace, and the whole mount quaked greatly."*

Hebrews 12:22-29 contrasts how the children of Israel went to Mount Sinai to meet with God, but we come to Mount Zion, which is used figuratively as a metaphor for the church. *"But ye are come unto mount Sion, and unto the city of the living God, the heavenly Jerusalem, and to an innumerable company of angels, To the general assembly and church of the firstborn, which are written in heaven, and to God the Judge of all, and to the spirits of just men made perfect, And to Jesus the mediator of the new covenant, and to the blood of sprinkling, that speaketh better things than that of Abel. See that ye refuse not him that speaketh. For if they escaped not who refused him that spake on earth, much more shall not we escape, if we turn away from him that speaketh from heaven: Whose voice then shook the earth: but now he hath promised, saying, Yet once more I shake not the earth only, but also heaven. And this word, Yet once more, signifieth the removing of those things that are shaken, as of things that are made, that those things which cannot be shaken may remain. Wherefore we receiving a kingdom which cannot be moved, let us have grace, whereby we may serve God acceptably with reverence and godly fear: **For our God is a consuming fire**."*

What they entered into was a heavenly Jerusalem and a spiritual kingdom, a kingdom that cannot be shaken. (I will write more on that in my next book.) Notice the similarities between the first Pentecost and the fulfillment in Acts 2. At the first Pentecost, the fire of God came down on Mount Sinai and the voice of God spoke out of the mountain. In the upper room, the fire of God fell on the 120 believers and the voice of God spoke through them via the gift of tongues.

Consider these comparisons and contrasts between the original Pentecost at Mt. Sinai (Ex. 19) and the spiritual fulfillment in the upper room (Ac. 2):

The first Pentecost was the birth of Judaism; Pentecost in Acts 2 was the birth of the New Covenant Church.

- The Israelites gathered at Mt. Sinai; the disciples came to Mt. Zion (a figurative metaphor for the church—Heb. 12:18-24).

- The first Pentecost was the birth of Judaism; Pentecost in Acts 2 was the birth of the New Covenant Church.

- At Mt. Sinai, the Israelites were sanctified for three days in preparation for God's visitation (Ex. 19:10-11, 14-15); in the upper room, the disciples tarried in prayer for about a week before the Holy Spirit arrived (Ac. 1:14-15).

- The fire of God fell on Mt. Sinai (Ex. 19:18); cloven tongues of fire appeared on the disciples (Ac. 2:3).

- God's audible voice spoke from Mt. Sinai the 10 Commandments (Ex. 19:19; 20:1, 27); God spoke through the disciples via tongues the wonderful works of God (Ac. 2:4-11).

- Supernatural signs indicated God's presence on Mt. Sinai (a cloud, thunder, lightning, fire and smoke—Ex. 19:16, 18); in Jerusalem, they heard a sound from heaven as a mighty wind (the breath of God) when the Spirit filled the house (Ac. 2:2).

- An earthquake shook Mt. Sinai with the glory of God (Ex. 19:18); the disciples staggered under the influence of the Spirit and bystanders thought they were drunk on new wine (Ac. 2:13, 15).

- At Mt. Sinai, the Mosaic Covenant was established, written on tables of stone; in Acts 2, the New Covenant was established, written on the tables of their hearts (2 Cor. 3:3, Heb. 8:10).

- At Mt. Sinai, the Levitical Priesthood was instituted after the golden calf idolatry (Ex. 32:26-29); at Pentecost, the priesthood of all believers became reality (1 Pt. 2:9).

- At Mt. Sinai, God gave Moses the blueprint for the Tabernacle (Ex. 25-31); at Pentecost, God gave the apostles the plan for the church (Ac. 2:14-18).

- At Mt. Sinai, 3,000 rebels who worshipped the golden calf were killed (Ex. 32:28); at Pentecost, 3,000 repentant sinners were saved (Ac. 2:37-41).

- At Mt. Sinai, the Law was given; in the upper room, the Holy Spirit was given.

Looking back to the "fire" in Acts 2, remember they saw something that looked like fire. Fire purifies and consumes the chaff. *"Whose fan is in his hand, and he will throughly purge his floor, and gather his wheat into the garner; but he will burn up the chaff with unquenchable fire"* (Matthew 3:12). The chaff represents the flesh or remnants of the old man. Look at the parallels in this verse, fan (wind), floor (upper room), wheat (Pentecost or Feast of Harvest), the harvest of the wheat (believers), consuming fire (tongues of fire). All the disciples were experiencing the same thing Jeremiah experienced, *"Then I said, I will not make mention of him, nor speak any more in his name. But* **his word was in mine heart as a burning fire shut up in my bones***, and I was weary with forbearing, and I could not stay"* (Jeremiah 20:9). From this day forward, the Words of Jesus were like fire in their bones. We need a fresh baptism of Holy Spirit fire. Our God is a consuming fire. A consuming fire, if it is set on any item, will not be quenched without fully consuming that item. *"For the Lord thy God is a consuming fire, even a jealous God"* (Deuteronomy 4:24). *"For our God is a consuming fire"* (Hebrews 12:29). Incidentally, when God spoke to a man (Moses), He lit a bush on fire; when He spoke to a nation (Israel), He lit a whole mountain on fire! The Holy Spirit is a consuming fire. Now read the verse that follows Hebrews 12:29, *"Let brotherly love continue"* (Hebrews 13:1). The only thing left after the consuming fire is a pure, brotherly love.

Some ask, "Is speaking in tongues for everyone?" I believe the answer is "yes." Peter announced who the promise of Spirit baptism was intended for in Acts 2:39, *"For the promise is unto you, and to your children, and to all that are afar off, even as many as the Lord our God shall call."* On three occasions in the book of Acts, receiving of the Holy Spirit was accompanied by speaking in tongues:

1. **The 120 believers in the upper room on the Day of Pentecost**: *"And they were all filled with the Holy Ghost, and* **began to speak with other tongues***, as the Spirit gave them utterance"*—Acts 2:4.

2. **Cornelius' household in Caesarea**: *"While Peter yet spake these words, the Holy Ghost fell on all*

*them which heard the word. And they of the circumcision which believed were astonished, as many as came with Peter, because that on the Gentiles also was poured out the gift of the Holy Ghost. For t***hey heard them speak with tongues**, *and magnify God"*—Acts 10:44-46.

3. **The Ephesian believers**: *"And when Paul had laid his hands upon them, the Holy Ghost came on them; and* **they spake with tongues**, *and prophesied"*—Acts 19:6.

Some ask if speaking in tongues is the evidence of receiving the Holy Spirit. My answer is no, but it is usually the initial sign of Spirit baptism. The true evidence is the fruit of the Spirit. *"But the fruit of the Spirit is love, joy, peace, longsuffering, gentleness, goodness, faith, Meekness, temperance: against such there is no law"* (Galatians 5:22-23). Please pastors, never forbid speaking in tongues. To do so would contradict Paul's instruction in 1 Corinthians 14:39, *"Wherefore, brethren, covet to prophesy, and* **forbid not to speak with tongues**.*"* To those of you that manifest the gift of tongues, don't let your flesh get involved. It must be done decently and in order. The Holy Spirit came because of obedience and tongues followed His indwelling. Obedience puts us in a receptive position. *"And we are his witnesses of these things; and so is also the Holy Ghost, whom God hath given to them that obey him"* (Acts 5:32). Acts 8:14-17 records how Peter and John were sent to pray for the Samaritans who believed and were saved under the preaching of Philip to receive the Holy Spirit *"Now when the apostles which were at Jerusalem heard that Samaria had received the word of God, they sent unto them Peter and John: Who, when they were come down, prayed for them, that they might receive the*

Holy Ghost: (For as yet he was fallen upon none of them: only they were baptized in the name of the Lord Jesus.) Then laid they their hands on them, and they received the Holy Ghost." This passage informs us that the baptism of the Holy Spirit and the gift of tongues are an experience that comes after salvation.

Acts 19:2-6 also proves that Spirit baptism is comes after salvation *"He said unto them,* **Have ye received the Holy Ghost since ye believed***? And they said unto him, We have not so much as heard whether there be any Holy Ghost. And he said unto them, Unto what then were ye baptized? And they said, Unto John's baptism. Then said Paul, John verily baptized with the baptism of repentance, saying unto the people, that they should believe on him which should come after him, that is, on Christ Jesus. When they heard this, they were baptized in the name of the Lord Jesus. And when Paul had laid his hands upon them, the Holy Ghost came on them; and they spake with tongues, and prophesied."*

I thought these scriptures were important to mention again because the sign given that they received the Holy Spirit was speaking in tongues. But the real evidence of the infilling comes later with the fruit of the Spirit. Speaking in tongues is the first or initial manifestation or sign of the infilling of the Holy Spirit. I say it this way because I have seen people fake speaking in tongues, but you can't fake the fruit of the Spirit. In fact, Paul wrote in 1 Corinthians 13:1-2 that the gifts of the Spirit (tongues, prophecy, knowledge, faith, etc.) without the fruit of the Spirit (love) are worthless. *"Though I speak with the tongues of men and of angels, and have not charity, I am become as sounding brass, or a tinkling cymbal. And though I have the gift of prophecy, and understand all mysteries, and all knowledge; and though I have all faith, so that I could remove mountains, and have not charity, I am nothing."* Again, when the Holy Spirit burns off the chaff, the only thing left is love—Christ's love working through us. All the scriptures where the Bible records people speaking in tongues are connected to people being filled with the Holy Spirit.

Some people use the following verses against those who speak in an unknown tongue, *"And there were dwelling at Jerusalem Jews, devout men, out of every nation under heaven. Now when this was noised abroad, the multitude came together, and were confounded, because that every man heard them speak in his own language. And they were all amazed and marvelled, saying one to another, Behold, are not all these which speak Galilaeans? And how hear we every man in our own tongue, wherein we were born?"* (Acts 2:5-8). Thousands of foreigners crowded the streets of Jerusalem to celebrate the Feast of Pentecost. These visitors spoke many different languages. The Holy Spirit enabled the 120 Galilean disciples to supernaturally translate the Gospel into all of those languages "the wonderful works of God."

In Acts 2:14-15, Peter explained to the crowd what was going on, *"But Peter, standing up with the eleven, lifted up his voice, and said unto them, Ye men of Judaea, and all ye that dwell at Jerusalem, be this known unto you, and hearken to my words: For these are not drunken, as ye suppose, seeing it is but the third hour of the day."* Peter stood up with the eleven to preach. They were all still in one accord. Peter raised or lifted up his voice. He was filled with courage and boldness, unlike when he denied Jesus before being filled with the Holy Spirit on about fifty-three days earlier. Peter didn't do as the Rabbis of that day who would sit down and instruct those listening. Peter stood and boldly proclaimed the truth. Critics and skeptics tried to discredit this move of God by saying they were just all drunk. *"Others mocking said, These men are full of new wine"* (Acts 2:13). Peter communicated that it was not even thinkable for people to be so drunken that early in the day; the third hour is nine o'clock in the morning. The custom of the Jews was not to eat or drink anything until after the "Hour of Prayer," which is when the Holy Spirit filled the house. This is seen in Acts 3:1 when Peter and John went to the Temple at the "hour of prayer, being the ninth hour" or nine o'clock in the morning.

PETER'S PENTECOST SERMON

Peter went on to explain that what they were witnessing was the fulfillment of prophecy, *"But this is that which was spoken by the prophet Joel;* **And it shall come to pass in the last days, saith God, I will pour out of my Spirit upon all flesh**: *and your sons and your daughters shall prophesy, and your young men shall see visions, and your old men shall dream dreams: And on my servants and on my handmaidens I will pour out in those days of my Spirit; and they shall prophesy: And I will shew wonders in heaven above, and signs in the earth beneath; blood, and fire, and vapour of smoke: The sun shall be turned into darkness, and the moon into blood, before the great and notable day of the Lord come: And it shall come to pass, that whosoever shall call on the name of the Lord shall be saved"* (Acts 2:16-21).

"I will pour out of my Spirit upon all flesh."

In the middle of this great outpouring of the Holy Spirit with signs, wonders, and speaking in tongues, Peter paused and said, "Let's turn to the book of Joel." I hear some people say, "We had a great service, and nobody even preached." This bothers me. All the signs, wonders, and speaking in tongues were preparing them for what Peter was about to share from God's Word, which, by the way, resulted in a huge altar call that added to them three thousand souls. Some think it is more spiritual if there is no Word preached. Others think if the Word is brought forth and there are no signs and wonders, then they are more spiritual or mature. They are both wrong. The Spirit and the Word agree, and we need both the preaching of the Word and the manifestation of the Spirit.

Peter quoted from the prophet Joel, *"And it shall come to pass afterward, that I will pour out my spirit upon all flesh; and your sons and your daughters shall prophesy, your old men shall dream dreams, your young men shall see visions: And also upon the servants and upon the handmaids in those days will I pour out my spirit. And I will shew wonders in the heavens and in the earth, blood, and fire, and pillars of smoke. The sun shall be turned into darkness, and the moon into blood, before the great and terrible day of the Lord come. And it shall come to pass, that whosoever shall call on the name of the Lord shall be delivered: for in mount Zion and in Jerusalem shall be deliverance, as the Lord hath said, and in the remnant whom the Lord shall call"* (Joel 2:28-32).

Part of this prophecy was fulfilled on the Day of Pentecost with the other part to be fulfilled in the last days with the second coming of Jesus. The Prophet Joel said, "It shall come to pass afterwards," while Peter said, "This is that which was spoken by the Prophet Joel." This was a glorious message brought forth on the Day of Pentecost. Under the Old Covenant, only certain people were moved upon with the Spirit at various times for specific purposes. Now, under the New Covenant, the outpouring of the Holy Spirit is for everyone who calls upon the name of the LORD!

Let's look at the rest of Peter's Pentecost sermon. I recommend you take a few minutes to read through the whole thing: *"Ye men of Israel, hear these words; Jesus of Nazareth, a man approved of God among you by miracles and wonders and signs, which God did by him in the midst of you, as ye yourselves also know: Him, being delivered by the determinate counsel and foreknowledge of God, ye have taken, and by wicked hands have crucified and slain: Whom God hath raised up, having loosed the pains of death: because it was not possible that he should be holden of it. For David speaketh concerning him, I foresaw the Lord always before my face, for he is on my right hand, that I should not be moved: Therefore did my heart rejoice, and my tongue was glad; moreover also my flesh shall rest in hope: Because thou wilt not leave my soul in hell, neither wilt thou suffer thine Holy One to see corruption. Thou hast made known to me the ways of life; thou shalt make me full of joy with thy countenance. Men and brethren, let me freely speak unto you of the patriarch David, that he is both dead and buried, and his sepulchre is with us unto this day. Therefore being a prophet, and knowing that God had sworn with an oath to him, that of the fruit of his loins, according to the flesh, he would raise up Christ to sit on his throne; He seeing this before spake of the resurrection of Christ, that his soul was not left in hell, neither his flesh did see corruption. This Jesus hath God raised up, whereof we all are witnesses. Therefore being by the right hand of God exalted, and having received of the Father the promise of the Holy*

Ghost, he hath shed forth this, which ye now see and hear. For David is not ascended into the heavens: but he saith himself, The Lord said unto my Lord, Sit thou on my right hand, Until I make thy foes thy footstool. Therefore let all the house of Israel know assuredly, that God hath made the same Jesus, whom ye have crucified, both Lord and Christ. Now when they heard this, they were pricked in their heart, and said unto Peter and to the rest of the apostles, Men and brethren, what shall we do. Then Peter said unto them, Repent, and be baptized every one of you in the name of Jesus Christ for the remission of sins, and ye shall receive the gift of the Holy Ghost. For the promise is unto you, and to your children, and to all that are afar off, even as many as the Lord our God shall call. And with many other words did he testify and exhort, saying, Save yourselves from this untoward generation. Then they that gladly received his word were baptized: and the same day there were added unto them about three thousand souls" (Acts 2:22-41).

Peter was preaching to unbelievers. Jesus had clearly given the disciples a mandate to preach the Gospel to the whole world for the salvation of souls. *"And Jesus came and spake unto them, saying, All power is given unto me in heaven and in earth. Go ye therefore, and teach all nations, baptizing them in the name of the Father, and of the Son, and of the Holy Ghost: Teaching them to observe all things whatsoever I have commanded you: and, lo, I am with you always, even unto the end of the world. Amen"* (Matthew 28:18-20). *"And he said unto them, Go ye into all the world, and preach the gospel to every creature. He that believeth and is baptized shall be saved; but he that believeth not shall be damned. And these signs shall follow them that believe; In my name shall they cast out devils; they shall speak with new tongues; They shall take up serpents; and if they drink any deadly thing, it shall not hurt them; they shall lay hands on the sick, and they shall recover. So then after the Lord had spoken unto them, he was received up into heaven, and sat on the right hand of God. And they went forth, and preached every where, the Lord working with them, and confirming the word with signs following. Amen"* (Mark 16:15-20).

Pentecost is often called the "birthday of the church" because it was on that day the apostles, strengthened by the Holy Spirit, started to preach the Gospel of Jesus Christ to the whole world. Notice that the responsibility of the church isn't to make people feel comfortable about themselves or even simply to exhort our fellow Christians. Our main responsibility is going out in the streets and preaching the Gospel to people who are not already saved. Peter quoted extensively from the Scriptures in his sermon. We must stay in the Word to fulfil Christ's mandates. Peter preached from the Old Testament; the New Testament was not written yet. Some preachers today refuse to preach from the Old Testament, but I would like to point something out. Not only is it just as inspired as the New Testament, but the Old Testament preaches about and points us toward Christ and is indispensable for understanding the Gospel of Jesus Christ in its fullness. Even Jesus said in Matthew 5:17, *"Think not that I am come to destroy the law, or the prophets: I am not come to destroy, but to fulfil."*

Peter openly confronted them with their sin. Notice Acts 2:23 again, *"Him, being delivered by the determinate counsel and foreknowledge of God, ye have taken, and by wicked hands have crucified and slain."* Peter declared unto them in verse 36, *"God hath made that same Jesus, whom ye have crucified, both Lord and Christ."* Modern day preachers might say that Peter was being too harsh, thinking that openly pointing out the people's sin and its consequences would surely turn people off to Jesus. They might think Peter should have stayed positive and only talked about how much Jesus loved them. Please listen, unless you understand that you are sinner that needs saving you cannot accept the Gospel! Salvation from our sins is precisely what the Gospel is! Jesus' very name means "God saves," or "Jehovah is salvation" in Hebrew. The angel explained to Joseph why He was given this name. *"And she shall bring forth a son, and thou shalt call his name Jesus: for* **he shall save his people from their sins***"* (Matthew 1:21). If people don't know they are sinners in desperate need of God's grace for salvation, then it won't be clear why they need Jesus at all in the first place.

After hearing Peter clearly preach about their sinfulness and about Christ's death, resurrection, and ascension into heaven, Peter replied, *"Repent, and be baptized every one of you in the name of Jesus Christ for the remission of sins, and ye shall receive the gift of the Holy Ghost"* (Acts 2.38). Peter told them to do two things: to repent from their sins, and to be baptized. After explaining what they needed to do, Scripture tells us, *"And with many other words did he testify and exhort, saying, Save yourselves from this untoward generation"* (Acts 2:40). Peter didn't spend any time trying to win people over by telling them how great they were. This world is fallen, and the life Christ calls us to demands change.

If you are living the way most people around you are living, you are probably not following Jesus. This is why Peter preached, "Save yourselves from this untoward (corrupt) generation." After Peter's sermon, 3,000 people were converted in one day. *"Then they that gladly received his word were baptized: and the same day there were added unto them about three thousand souls"* (Acts 2:41).

WHAT THE DISCIPLES DID AFTER PENTECOST

Finally, let's gain some understanding of Acts 2:42-47, *"And they continued stedfastly in the apostles' doctrine and fellowship, and in breaking of bread, and in prayers. And fear came upon every soul: and many wonders and signs were done by the apostles. And all that believed were together, and had all things common; And sold their possessions and goods, and parted them to all men, as every man had need. And they, continuing daily with one accord in the temple, and breaking bread from house to house, did eat their meat with gladness and singleness of heart, Praising God, and having favour with all the people. And the Lord added to the church daily such as should be saved."*

> *"And they continued stedfastly in the apostles' doctrine and fellowship, and in breaking of bread, and in prayers."*

After Pentecost, what did they do? "They continued steadfastly ..." The Greek word *proskartereoreō* can mean "to be earnest, to persevere, to be constantly diligent or to adhere closely to." This is the same word that Luke used to describe the activities of the disciples following Jesus' ascension when he wrote, *"These all continued with one accord in prayer"* (Acts 1:14). Then, after Pentecost, "they continued stedfastly in the apostles' doctrine and fellowship, and in breaking of bread, and in prayers" (Acts 2:42).

They continued in the apostles' doctrine. You may ask, "what is the apostles' doctrine?" The word "doctrine" derives from the Latin term for teaching. It refers to the content that was taught in the New Testament. The proper teaching of Scripture was called "The Apostles Doctrine," meaning that which the apostles taught. They only taught what Jesus taught them. The apostles' doctrine is true not because an apostle said it, but because it is "consistent" with the what the whole Word of God says.

The Bereans examined the teachings of Paul in light of the Scriptures before accepting it. *"And the brethren immediately sent away Paul and Silas by night unto Berea: who coming thither went into the synagogue of the Jews. These were more noble than those in Thessalonica, in that* **they received the word with all readiness of mind***,* **and searched the scriptures daily***, whether those things were so. Therefore many of them believed; also of honourable women which were Greeks, and of men, not a few"* (Acts 17:10-12). They also continued in "fellowship." The term Luke uses for fellowship is a much broader term than our English word. Essentially, fellowship means "joint participation" or "sharing something in common." It is thus a kind of partnership. *"If there be therefore any consolation in Christ, if any comfort of love, if any* **fellowship of the Spirit***, if any bowels and mercies, Fulfil ye my joy, that ye be likeminded, having the same love, being of one accord, of one mind"* (Philippians 2:1-2). The term used for fellowship is a common sharing together in the Holy Spirit.

The apostles also broke bread from house to house. They continued in the breaking of bread and in prayers. This "breaking of bread" was included with the teaching and the prayers. It's an activity of faith and worship to which they devoted themselves. It is clear that "breaking of bread" in that context is a reference to the Communion or Lord's Supper that Jesus instituted the night He was betrayed. We find this also mentioned in Acts 2:46, *"And they, continuing daily with one accord in the temple, and **breaking bread from house to house**, did eat their meat with gladness and singleness of heart."* Here the disciples' "breaking bread" is defined as eating meals in fellowship together. So, in the early church, we find them "breaking bread" in two distinct activities—sharing meals and observing the Lord's Supper.

Finally, we will end this study with this verse, *"Praising God, and having favour with all the people. And the Lord added to the church daily such as should be saved"* (Acts 2:47). I long to see Acts 2 fulfilled in the church again. And I believe we will see this again as we personally and corporately take to heart the truths, the principles, and love with which I presented them to you. Thanks for reading this book. I hope and pray you have been blessed!

CONCLUSION
by Brad Bartlett

The journey through this book has challenged my theology, my thinking, and my walk with the Lord. Doctor Fred Stapleton, or "Freddie" as most call him, charged me with helping move this book from draft to manuscript. Having myself hungered and thirsted for righteousness for twenty-eight years, this book has put some icing on the cake of my Christianity. The cake has not yet been decorated because, like every one of us, I am a work in progress. Many of us have had those times when we suddenly see how various truths fit together and give revelation and growth in our beliefs and spiritual walk. This book has provided multiple opportunities to have "Ah ha!" moments. Fred ties Scripture together with supporting Scripture and creates those "shofar trumpet blasts" of God's call to righteousness in our hearts. It has been my pleasure to be a link in the chain for the presentation of the many valuable treasures presented in this book. I pray they have further equipped you to hear and follow the call of God to life and life more abundantly—a life filled to overflowing with fruit that remains.

The chapters of John 13 through Acts 2 paint an intricate and complete picture of the New Covenant. These Scriptures describe in detail both our rights and our responsibilities as we aspire to be used by God. Simplified, our right is to be called children of God because of His shed blood and our belief in the truth of Jesus Christ. Our responsibility, or our part in allowing these truths to become real, is to believe and turn away from everything related to the flesh so we may truly be led by the Spirit. In other words, let truth transform your behavior and thought life to align with Scripture to the point it is evident to all that you are led by the Spirit. This book has given you scriptural equipping and clarification of the Lord's provision and His expectations for true believers.

The term "true believers" is used because if we honestly look at churches today, many are generally sick and emaciated compared to the early church Jesus gave birth to. This book solidifies the core reasons and causes for this being true. Hopefully, you have walked step by step to a higher calling, a new level of purity, and a greater effectiveness in the cause of Christ by reading this book. Now let us become doers of these words and not just hearers of these words. Do not be a make-believer who deceives himself by thinking intellectual acceptance of truth is the same as application of truth. In this information age we live in, too many have allowed knowledge to puff them up to the point of ineffectiveness. We have more programs, more mega churches, and more opinions on effective evangelism than ever before yet, generally, our churches are populated with either immature believers, or those who are in this to make themselves look good, or even worse, those who just want the "fire insurance!" These are make believers which have caused the name of our God to be blasphemed among the Gentiles.

What is the solution to the pandemic of apostasy? For me, the solution has been found in Fred's book. The solution has come through a clearer understanding of just what God actually did for us on the cross and what God has commissioned and equipped us to be. This understanding is combined with the realization of this fact—we will not have an end-time revival and outpouring of God's Spirit without a major, real time growth in the maturity of Christians. This growing will permit the power of God to be manifest to a lost and dying world through us. It requires the death of our flesh, which is our sacrifice and the indwelling of His Spirit which is given to us by His sacrifice. Let us be washed with the Word and purified in our souls so that we may demonstrate our salvation and save multitudes. The fields are white unto harvest.

In summary, if this book has touched and motivated you, share it, recommend it, teach from its Bible-based truth, and even preach these revival-producing concepts in your pulpits. As for me, I will never be the same. I have been edified, strengthened, and equipped to go where I have never been before. Personally, my soul is filled with the initial joy of my salvation. My prayer is that revival has happened for you as well. Remember, Christianity is caught by the invitation of the Spirit. Then it is properly taught by men filled with Spirit and Truth. Fred Stapleton is one of those men.

Through Christ's Love,

Brad Bartlett

PHOTO GALLERY

A mission trip to the country of Belize, Central America, in 1992

A mission trip to Kenya in 1994

Our missionary team in Nairobi, Kenya

Our missionary teams to East Poket, Kenya

PHOTO GALLERY

This young man, David, was found in a garden after an earthquake separated him from his family. My daughter Bekah is currently trying to adopt him and bring him to the USA.

Bekah Soots and David

Ralston and Bekah Soots and David

*My daughter Bekah Lynn
in East Pokey, Kenya*

Special school friends in Lusaka, Zambia

School friend in Zambia

This woman was miraculously healed after Connie prayed for her.

Connie and I at Living Stone Church in Lusaka, Zambia

PHOTO GALLERY

This little boy was given up to die at four months old.

This is a picture of him at ten years old.

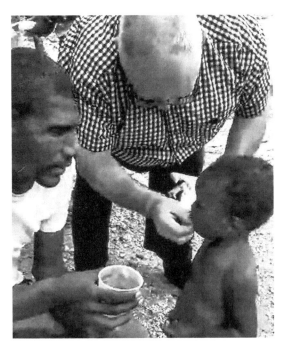

Feeding my little friend in the Dominican Republic

Anna, Candice and Bekah in The Gambia

PHOTO GALLERY

Ambassadors Joshua and Ashley Tallent

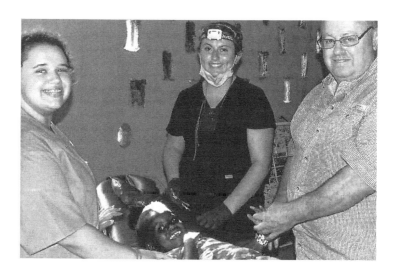

During a mission trip to Haiti, we met this little girl. She had four abscessed teeth. The dentist could not numb them, but after prayer all the pain was gone, and he was able to remove the teeth.

This a school we support in Haiti, through our Covenant Christian World Mission (CCWM). It has over 300 children.

My daughter, Priscilla Ann, in Romania

My daughter, Joy Danielle, in Haiti